THE OFFICIAL

AMAZING RACE

TRAVEL COMPANION

THE OFFICIAL

AMAZING RACE

TRAVEL COMPANION

MORE THAN
20 YEARS OF ROADBLOCKS, DETOURS, AND REAL-LIFE ACTIVITIES TO EXPERIENCE AROUND THE GLOBE

ELISE DOGANIERI

SIMON ELEMENT

New York   London   Toronto   Sydney   New Delhi

**SIMON
ELEMENT**

An Imprint of Simon & Schuster, Inc.
1230 Avenue of the Americas
New York, NY 10020

First Simon Element trade paperback edition October 2022

SIMON ELEMENT is a trademark of Simon & Schuster, Inc.

For information about special discounts for bulk purchases, please
contact Simon & Schuster Special Sales at 1-866-506-1949
or business@simonandschuster.com.

The Simon & Schuster Speakers Bureau can bring authors to your live event.
For more information or to book an event, contact the Simon & Schuster Speakers
Bureau at 1-866-248-3049 or visit our website at www.simonspeakers.com.

Interior design by Laura Levatino

Manufactured in the United States of America

10 9 8 7 6 5 4 3 2 1

Library of Congress Cataloging-in-Publication Data has been applied for.

ISBN 978-1-9821-7739-3
ISBN 978-1-9821-7741-6 (ebook)

I dedicate this book to my loving and supportive parents, Lorraine and Michael Doganieri.

Thank you for inspiring me, encouraging me, and, most of all, believing in me.

I will forever miss your *Amazing Race*–themed dinner parties inspired by the culture, food, and traditions of each country we traveled to during the season.

I miss you both every day; you are always with me.

Contents

Foreword   ix
Introduction   xiii
Tips, Packing, and More!   xvii
Clue Key   xx

North America   1
South America   27
Europe   39
Africa   73
Middle East   91
Asia   101
Oceania   131

Behind the Scenes   145
Acknowledgments   157
Notes   159
Index   181

To move, to breathe, to fly, to float,
To gain all while you give,
To roam the roads of lands remote,
To travel is to live.

—Hans Christian Andersen

FOREWORD

I recently found a Kodachrome slide of my great-uncle Morris carrying me across the tarmac to board an NAC Boeing 737 with my family. I was almost three. My parents had decided to leave New Zealand to take on a new adventure in Guelph, a small university town in Canada. At the time I was blissfully unaware that my first trip to the other side of the world would lead to a lifetime of travel. Now, whenever I see a plane in the sky, I can't help but wonder where its lucky passengers are heading, and always wish I was with them.

Over more than fifty years I've had the privilege of visiting more than 130 countries, many of them dozens of times. I'm often asked where my favorite place is. New Zealand has to be up there; I love any opportunity to get home and be with family. Italy also ranks highly, because it has all the ingredients I like for a good trip: fantastic history, culture, wine, food, and people. The truth is, I really think my favorite place to visit is a place I've never visited before.

I love planning adventures, researching where to go and what to do before packing my bags. Preparing for a trip allows you to extend the journey and maximize your time once you get there. I walked the Old Ghost Road through the Southern Alps with my dad a few years back, and some of my fondest memories of the trip were of us poring over maps of the terrain we were going to face in the weeks leading up to our hike.

If time isn't a factor, there's also something wonderful about having absolutely no clue what lies ahead of you. Jumping in headfirst offers a chance to venture into the unknown, get lost on purpose, and let randomness take over.

Back in the late 1990s, I set out to meet the Yukuana people of Venezuela. After landing in Caracas, I jumped in a small plane and flew into the heart of the Venezuelan jungle. We touched down on a dirt runway, and I headed to the very end of a long, winding dirt road in a four-by-four; at that point I found myself "off the map." This was where I met a local biologist named John, who had arranged for us to travel upriver in a dugout canoe. After a four-hour trip we were met by the Yukuana chief, who kindly invited us to stay with him and his family for a few days. I decided to completely let go of my agenda and allow myself to be fully immersed in the ways of the Yukuana people. The majority of our time was spent hunting and gathering, and while I'm not 100 percent sure about everything I ate during my stay, I now know that green ants in leaves mixed with spiderwebs taste like citrus, and grilled piranha is surprisingly delicious. I'm glad to say the hundred-pound capybara we were hunting got away; while I'm up for just about anything, eating the world's largest rodent was *not* exactly something I felt I needed to add to my to-do list!

Traveling extensively all through my childhood with my plant-scientist father and music-teacher mother, I was taught that wherever you go in the world, you're a guest, and just like visiting someone's house, it's important to be respectful of others' customs. If they would prefer you take your shoes off at the door, don't argue. Treat people with respect, and you're almost guaranteed to be treated the same way. If you're being hosted, let that person take the lead; step back a bit and take in what's going on around you. Pay careful attention to the way people dress—if you're in doubt about what to wear, ask. Make an attempt at the local language and customs; try to blend in and fly under the radar. Ask yourself: Am I being too loud or pulling out my camera at the wrong time? While it's impossible to get everything right, always try your best not to be offensive in any way.

My mind is filled with incredible memories of the places and adventures I've been fortunate enough to enjoy: mining in Coober Pedy,

Australia, the opal capital of the world; diving with hundreds of whale sharks off the coast of Mexico; getting my reindeer racing license in Finland's Arctic Circle; having a five-star meal on top of the Mount Stromboli volcano during an eruption; putting a golf ball from coast to coast across Scotland and ending on the eighteenth green at St Andrews; breaking an unofficial bungee-jumping world record with eight other crazies in Queenstown, New Zealand; exploring the world's longest underwater caves below the jungle on the Yucatán Peninsula; riding my bike across America and later circumnavigating France on an eighty-five-year-old Tour de France bicycle . . . hundreds of adventures, millions of miles, dozens of trips around the world, and ultimately what I remember most are the people I've met along the way.

If I can give you any advice about travel, it's that you should make an effort to meet the locals—don't lock yourself away in a hotel. Find out where the best eating spots or food trucks are, and the best places to get coffee or fresh fruit, or even where the favorite watering holes are. You will be blown away by the kindness of strangers, and you never know— you may make enduring friendships along the way. Another great way to connect with people is to reach out to those who share your interests. My family met lifelong friends when a couple reached out to my mother to play music. For years, they would travel the world and connect with local musicians to play classical pieces. While they weren't always able to speak the same verbal language, they were able to share the international language of music.

The more I travel, the more I realize I still have so much to learn. Your passport can literally open up a world of surprises—don't be scared to get out there and explore. You'll quickly realize that people all over this planet are searching for the same things: better lives for themselves and their children, and connection with other humans. You never know—that might mean you.

When I set out on my first *Amazing Race* adventure, I wanted to say something that would capture the promise of what was to come, and that was when I first uttered the line "The world is waiting for you!" It was then, and it is now!

Live while you still have a chance: swerve off that predictable road you've been following for years and connect with people you don't know—beginning with yourself! Go on, get out there and "Tick it before you kick it!"

—**Phil Keoghan**

INTRODUCTION

W e are so thrilled to share with you some of the incredible places we have traveled to on *The Amazing Race* so that you might use this book as a guide to plan out your next big adventure (or use it as a launching point if you already have a trip planned and need some inspiration!). We have certainly traveled far and wide and chosen some of our most epic locations, which you will now be able to check out here in this book. But it's only fair to give you a little background on how it all began.

I was born in New York and had a very happy childhood with my loving parents, Lorraine and Michael, and my sister, Renée. In 1986 I attended the Fashion Institute of Technology to study advertising and graphic design, and soon after graduating in 1990, I started a consulting and design firm. My husband, Bertram, who was born in the Netherlands, went to the University of Munich to study filmmaking and traveled the world directing and producing commercials and documentaries.

In March of 1995 we met by chance on Franklin Street in NYC. My design firm was on the ground floor of a Tribeca loft, and I used the walls to display local artists' work. Bertram (who was living in Los Angeles at the time) was filming a pilot for a new television series with a mutual friend of ours, and they needed a large painting for one of their scenes. Our friend told Bertram that I had several that might work.

I met Bertram at my studio to negotiate a rental price for the painting, but funnily enough, we could not agree on a number. But he did ask me to dinner, and that was the beginning of our relationship.

Two years later I sold my company and moved to Los Angeles to start fresh with Bertram. At the time, Bertram had sold a wildlife series to Paramount called *Wild Things*, and we worked together on the pilot;

we traveled to Alaska and Kenya for a few months, and I enjoyed every minute of it, but I was offered a job at a big advertising agency that I couldn't pass up. *Wild Things* went on to be successful, and I missed those days of traveling terribly. In the fall of 1999, Bertram went to a trade show, but nothing awed him. When he returned, I said, "I don't know why there's nothing new and exciting in television!" He laughed and said, "You think it's so easy? Why don't you come up with an idea. I'll give you five minutes!"

I said "Okay," and in that very moment, I thought of the backpacking trip through Europe I had taken with my college roommate. I had a very vivid memory of the crazy adventures we had been on that summer; traveling from NYC to Madrid, taking an overnight ferry to Ibiza, traveling on a Eurail pass throughout Europe, staying in hostels, trying to communicate without speaking the language, and doing it all with a backpack and very little money.

Midway through the trip we found ourselves in Rome, and I was eager to get up early and get going. We had made plans to get together with some friends we'd met on the train, but Laurie, who was super easygoing, had had it with my go, go, go attitude. I will never forget her saying: "This isn't Chevy Chase's *European Vacation*; why don't you do your own thing today and I'll do mine." So we took a break from each other that day and met in the evening for dinner, and all was good again.

But the flashback to that moment sparked an idea: a global travel adventure competition, where teams of two would race around the world competing in mental and physical challenges. With very little money, and most likely not speaking the native language, they would travel from country to country by plane, bus, boat, train, car, or taxi, immersing themselves in the culture by doing things the locals do. Sometimes teams would do tasks together, and sometimes they would do them separately, but taking on a nonstop, nearly monthlong competition together like this would definitely test their relationship!

Bertram had traveled the world and worked in just about every country an airplane, train, boat, or bus could get to, so I knew he could make this show a reality. For years he had developed relationships in countries around the world, and he has a special way of making the impossible possible (even in the most remote locations). With his global network of contacts, he had already built the infrastructure necessary for *The Amazing Race*, and that's the way we brought this show to life. Bertram sat there for a moment after hearing the idea and then said, "I love it. Write it up and we'll pitch it!"

Our agent at CAA suggested we meet with Bruckheimer Television executive Jonathan Littman, and we soon decided to work together. We pitched the show to CBS, ABC, NBC, and Fox. All the networks liked it, but CBS saw it as a franchise and a long-running series, so that is ultimately where we landed. With CBS green-lighting the show, I had to make a decision: Should I quit my job at the advertising agency to pursue this full-time? Bertram knew how unpredictable television could be (it was possible that the show would never air or only run one season) and recommended that I not quit my job. I spoke with my boss, and they allowed me to take a leave of absence. I would return after we were done filming.

Within a few months, Bertram and I had set up our production company, Worldrace Productions, and hired a full staff; with a small team of seasoned producers we headed out scouting locations. Everything happened so fast. I remember flying to Delhi, India, taking a train to Agra, and then there I was, standing in front of the Taj Mahal. It was surreal. In just a few months so much had changed, and I couldn't have been more excited.

We started filming in early 2001. We had our cast, which was about to take on an adventure like no other, and they had no idea what to expect (and honestly, neither did we!). I remember standing at the Bethesda Fountain in New York City when the bus pulled up with all of the teams, everyone filled with adrenaline and anticipation. The teams lined up in front of Phil, and he said the words "the world is waiting for you, GO!" And they were off in all directions with our incredible camera crews running alongside them. In that moment, we all realized that we had better get going because the teams were all ahead of us! That's pretty much how it goes—we as the producers are in our own race to stay ahead of the nonstop freight train of contestants. We have dealt with delayed or canceled flights, missed trains and slow buses, sandstorms, typhoons, snowstorms, broken-down vehicles, burned-out clutches, flat tires, and running out of gas. We have seen and experienced it all, and loved every minute of it.

The show premiered on September 5, 2001, and thirty-three seasons later, we couldn't be more excited to have had more than twenty years and counting on the air! Season after season, Bertram and I never lose the thrill of scouting locations and running around the world with the contestants. Our production company has nearly tripled in staff since season 1; we had no idea that first season just how many people it would take to run a machine this big!

One of the many things we love about *The Amazing Race* is that we have a chance to give back to the communities we visit. It's so rewarding when we can leave a community better than when we arrived. Oftentimes we have challenges where the teams can help as well, such as building school desks in small villages, painting schoolrooms, building roofs on homes, building nets and rigs for fishing villages, and donating to orphanages.

There are so many wonderful things that have come from *The Amazing Race*.

We hope that the show has opened the world to those who are unable to travel, and for those who can, we hope it has opened your hearts to finding a common bond with someone from another country with whom you may have never imagined having something in common.

We feel so fortunate to have created a series that inspires people to travel the world and brings joy to those who watch the show. We hope this travel guide will inspire you to go to places you never imagined or only dreamed of going. So get your passport and get going!

—Elise Doganieri and Bertram van Munster,
co-creators and executive producers of *The Amazing Race*

TIPS, PACKING, AND MORE!

I t's always important to make sure you're prepared, and I hope this list can function as a checklist for you when planning your next adventure!

Prior to Departure:

- Make sure to bring an ATM bank card, as it's an easy way to get local cash and you won't have to find a bank or go to a hotel (where the fees may be high).
- Taxi drivers typically only accept the currency of the country you're in, so convert at least $50 of local currency before you get there.
- Make a copy of your passport and ID and place it in a safe spot in case you lose your original.
- Check your passport expiration date prior to departure and make sure it's valid for six months from the date of your travel or you may not be allowed into the country you're traveling to.
- When you're planning your vacation, check to see what visas you might need to enter the country.
- Make sure you have the proper vaccinations before entering a country; you may have to show your yellow card (vaccination card) when you land.
- Write a list on a piece of paper or in your phone notes with names and numbers of emergency contacts and any of your medical history, conditions, or medications.

- Research the type of international electrical plugs you might need for the country you're visiting.
- If you're traveling alone, consider bringing a doorstop to place under your hotel room door when you go to sleep at night (for peace of mind).
- Consider traveling with a small suitcase that can fit in the overhead on the plane (even if it's a secondary bag), in case your luggage gets lost.

Packing Tips

- Bring all your daily medications, and make sure to pack extra—it may be difficult to find a pharmacy with your specific prescriptions.
- Create an emergency kit with travel-size pain medications, antibacterial hand gel and wipes, sunscreen, bug spray, and Pepto Bismol, as well as a small first-aid kit and a travel-size roll of toilet paper (you never know!).
- It's always smart to pack sunglasses and a hat to avoid sunburn.
- You would be surprised to know how much a neck pillow can save your sanity and provide extra comfort on long flights.
- Pack clothes that you can layer, so you can add or subtract as temperatures change. Bring a windbreaker with a hood, as it's perfect for rain and wind.
- Consider investing in noise-canceling headphones (or bring simple earplugs) and an eye mask for the plane.
- Pack a portable charger to charge your phone or other devices.
- Be sure to bring good walking shoes.
- Remember your camera for memorable pictures; sometimes the phone just doesn't cut it!

When You Arrive

- It's best not to get lost in a foreign place, so if you leave your hotel for a walk or a jog, always write down or take a photo of the name, address, and phone number. You would be surprised how many times I have arrived at a hotel and gone for a walk and forgotten the address or name of my hotel!
- Haggle at markets and bazaars. Don't settle on the first price; negotiating can sometimes get you a better deal.
- If you're traveling in a country that requires modest dress, make sure to cover your shoulders and knees. This happens predominantly in places of worship or sacred temples, and dressing appropriately and modestly is strongly advised to show respect.

Clue Key

Route Markers: These clues provide information for the team's next destination. The clue will let teams know where to travel, but it's up to them to figure out how to get there.

Detour: A Detour confronts teams with the choice of completing one of two tasks. Some tasks are more physical but can be completed faster, while other tasks can be less physically demanding and more mentally challenging but may take longer. Teams may switch tasks if they find their first choice too difficult.

Roadblock: A Roadblock is a task that must be completed by only one of the two team members. Each team will read a brief clue and must decide which team member will undertake the task before opening the fully sealed Roadblock clue. It's required that both team members perform the same number of Roadblocks in a season. Generally, there's only one Roadblock on each leg of the race.

Fast Forward: During certain legs of the race, there may be a Fast Forward pass located along the route. Although more than one team can compete for the Fast Forward pass, the first team to complete the task will win the pass. Winning the Fast Forward pass allows a team to proceed directly to the next Pit Stop without having to complete any other challenges or travel to any other locations before the Pit Stop.

Clue Key

Speed Bump: On a non-elimination leg, the team that arrives last at a Pit Stop may have to complete a Speed Bump task on the next leg of the race, a task no other team is required to complete, prior to continuing with the remainder of the leg.

U-Turn: A team may elect to cause any other team (that has yet to reach the U-Turn location) to complete both sides of a Detour challenge before proceeding with the rest of the leg.

Pit Stop: The final stop at the end of a leg. After teams complete all tasks such as Detours, Roadblocks, and Route Markers, they must make their way to the Pit Stop. Each Pit Stop is a mandatory rest period that allows teams to relax and recharge. The order of arrival is established based on when both members of a team arrive together at the Pit Stop, and the last team to arrive at the end of a leg may be eliminated.

Final Leg: Typically, three teams race to the finish line in the final episode after completing all tasks in the Final Leg. The first team to reach Phil wins $1 million!

THE OFFICIAL

AMAZING RACE

TRAVEL COMPANION

NORTH AMERICA

New York | NYC

☐ ### *Visit the Bethesda Fountain and Terrace*
Season 1, Episode 1, Starting Line

Eleven teams of two lined up in front of Bethesda Fountain for the start of season 1 and ran up the grand staircase to find transportation to get to JFK Airport.

Sitting in lower Bethesda Terrace, this neoclassical sculpture, designed by Emma Stebbins in 1868, is also known as *Angel of the Waters*, featuring an eight-foot bronze angel "who stands above four small cherubim representing health, purity, temperance, and peace."[1]

Address: 72 Terrace Drive, New York, NY 10021

Behind-the-Scenes Snapshot: The fountain's location in Central Park was a wonderful place where I could escape the high-energy pace of living in New York City. In the summer I would look for a "summer share"— a rental house in the Hamptons—with a group of friends. Every weekend there would be a mass exodus from Manhattan to the eastern end of Long Island for house parties and long days at the beach. I had always wanted to find a way to showcase the magnificent beach homes in the Hamptons, and in season 27, we found a stunning house on Dune Road for the finale. One of the highlights of that day was spending it with my father, Michael, who was one of the gentlemen standing on the beach while the teams built Adirondack chairs. When the task was complete, he handed the final clue to Kelsey and Joey before they raced to the finish line to win the competition.

How to get there: Fly into JFK, LaGuardia, or Newark Airport, and then you can take the subway, a bus, or a taxi.

☐ *Visit the United Nations Headquarters*
Season 21, Episode 12, Roadblock

Throughout the season, for each of the eight countries visited during the race, the words "hello" and "goodbye" were spoken to each team by the Pit Stop greeters in their native language. For the final Roadblock, one teammate had to remember these words (which were written on small banners) and raise them up the flagpole flying that country's flag.

One-hour guided tours are offered at the UN Headquarters, where you can learn about the work and history of the United Nations. If there are no meetings being held, you will be able to see the General Assembly Hall and Security Council Chamber. Additionally, special tours, such as the Children's Tour, the Focus on Women Tour, the Black History Tour, and the Garden Tour, are offered throughout the year.[2]

Address: 760 United Nations Plaza, New York, NY 10017

☐ *Eat a Slice at Lombardi's Pizza, the First Pizzeria in the United States*
Season 21, Episode 12, Route Marker

At Lombardi's, teams had to pick up and deliver ten pizzas with various toppings to three different addresses in Little Italy without being allowed to take any notes.

Lombardi's is widely accepted as America's first pizzeria, which began selling coal-oven pizza in 1905.[3] Their original Little Italy location is open seven days a week.

Address: 32 Spring Street, New York, NY 10012

☐ *Visit the Unisphere*
Season 1, Episode 13, Finish Line

The Unisphere is the world's largest globe representing the Earth. At 120 feet in diameter and weighing 350 tons, it was commissioned for the New York World's Fair of 1964–65.[4] Located at Flushing Meadows–Corona Park in Queens, the fourth-largest park in NYC at 897 acres, the Unisphere is one of many attractions, including a tennis center where the US Open is held, a zoo, a museum, and Citi Field (home of the New York Mets).

Address: 11101 Corona Avenue, Flushing, NY 11355

Behind-the-Scenes Snapshot: There were several reasons for choosing the Unisphere as the finish line for season 1 of *The Amazing Race*. We started the race in New York City because it's one of the most amazing cities in the world (and happens to be in my home state), but we also wanted to go completely around the globe and finish back in NYC. The Unisphere's giant globe felt like a fitting final Pit Stop, as it represented the thirty-five-thousand-mile, thirty-five-day circumnavigation of the globe we had just completed.

> OTHER NEW YORK MUST-SEES!
>
> • THE STATUE OF LIBERTY
> • BROOKLYN BRIDGE
> • TIMES SQUARE
> • WASHINGTON SQUARE PARK
> • THE HAMPTONS, LONG ISLAND

How to get there: Long Island Railroad, subway, bus, taxi, or car

Michigan | Detroit

☐ Visit the Bank Safes in the Basement of the Guardian Building
Season 31, Episode 12, Roadblock

One team member had to rappel face-first five hundred feet down the Guardian Building. On the way down, they had to look for a series of numbers that they would need to unlock a bank vault, along with specific turn-by-turn instructions listed next to each safe in the basement of the building to retrieve their next clue.

Completed in 1929, the building is one of the most significant and striking Art Deco skyscrapers in the world. The 150-foot-long main lobby features a large glass mosaic, murals, and marble fixtures. The vaulted ceiling was crafted of Rookwood pottery and tile that was hand-stenciled and hand-painted.[5]

Address: 500 Griswold Street, Suite 1600, Detroit, MI 48226

How to get there: Fly into Detroit Metropolitan Wayne County Airport and take a taxi or rent a car.

☐ Play a Game of Fowling at the Fowling Warehouse
Season 31, Episode 12, Route Marker

At Fowling Warehouse, teams had to play a game of Fowling. Team members had to stand at opposite ends of a lane, each of them behind ten bowling pins positioned in a traditional bowling layout, and throw a football toward their partner's pins and knock them all down to receive their next clue.

The game of Fowling was created in 2001 and is a hybrid of football, bowling, and horseshoes.[6] The Fowling Warehouse in Hamtramck has thirty Fowling lanes, a beer garden, and a stage for live music.[7]

Address: 3901 Christopher Street, Hamtramck, MI 48211

☐ *Take a Tour of Third Man Records*
Season 31, Episode 12, Route Marker

Teams had to properly press five two-tone vinyl records using *Race* colors. Once all the vinyl records had been correctly made, with a distinct line between colors and properly placed labels, the team received their next clue.

Third Man Records was launched in 2001 by musician Jack White, and in 2015 the Detroit location opened, with a record and novelties retail area, a performance area, a mastering studio, and a vinyl record pressing manufacturing facility. They offer tours of the state-of-the-art vinyl production facility in the heart of Detroit's historic Cass Corridor neighborhood.[8]

Address: 441 W Canfield Street, Detroit, MI 48201

☐ *Visit the Historic Fort Wayne*
Season 31, Episode 12, Finish Line

Finished in 1849, Historic Fort Wayne has served the city of Detroit through many eras of war, yet a shot has never been fired here in combat. The location of Fort Wayne on Detroit's riverfront became a vital induction center for Michigan troops preparing to enter into battle for "every US conflict from the Civil War to Vietnam."[9]

Address: 6325 West Jefferson Avenue, Detroit, MI 48209

> *OTHER DETROIT MUST-SEES!*
>
> * *HEIDELBERG PROJECT*
> * *MOTOWN MUSEUM*
> * *HART PLAZA*
> * *SUNSET POINT*

Illinois | Chicago

☐ *Visit the Historic Chicago Water Tower*

Season 29, Episode 12, Route Marker

Once in Chicago, teams took a train to the Chicago Water Tower and had to find their next clue in front of the tower.

The Chicago Water Tower is one of the city's most recognizable and cherished landmarks. Completed in 1869, the Gothic Revival structure was really only created to hide the city's water system, and housed a 135-foot iron standpipe that regulated the city's water pressure.[10] The Water Tower famously survived the Great Chicago Fire of 1871, one of few buildings to do so. Though other sections of the city, such as the south and west side, were untouched by the fire, the Water Tower "became a rallying point for the city" and "stood as a symbol for a city determined to rise from its own ashes."[11] Open to the public, and now housing the "City Gallery in the Historic Water Tower," the venue showcases the work of local photographers and artists.[12]

Address: City Gallery in the Historic Water Tower, 806 North Michigan Avenue, Chicago, IL 60611

How to get there: Fly into Chicago O'Hare International Airport and take a train, bus, taxi, or rent a car.

☐ Eat a Deep-Dish Slice at the Original Gino's East Pizza

Season 6, Episode 12, Route Marker

Teams took a taxi to Gino's East Pizzeria, where each team member had to eat half of a deep-dish pizza to receive their final clue.

The original Gino's East opened in 1966 and has since become one of Chicago's most popular pizza joints. The place was founded by two taxi drivers and a close friend, a trio who knew that a hit pizza spot would be a good investment on the Magnificent Mile, but they had nothing to do with creating the pizza recipe that would make the restaurant so famous.[13] Instead, the trio hired Alice Mae Redmond, "a woman who had developed the dough recipe at a competing pizza restaurant" and who would spend the next twenty-three years making the pizza that made Gino's East iconic.[14] The restaurant is also world-famous for their tradition of letting customers leave their graffiti mark on the restaurant walls.

Original Address, as seen on *The Amazing Race*: 633 North Wells Street, Chicago, IL 60654

New Location: 162 East Superior Street, Chicago, IL 60611

☐ Visit the World-Famous Wrigley Field

Season 29, Episode 12, Route Marker

At Wrigley Field, the teams had to recall their placements in each leg of the race. One team member went inside the press box while the other entered the stadium's hand-operated scoreboard, which displayed the locations of the previous eleven Pit Stops. Unable to see the locations displayed on the scoreboard, the team member inside the board had to install numbered signs in the proper locations to indicate their team's placement at each Pit Stop, guided by their partner giving instructions from the press box via one-way radio.

Wrigley Field, home of the Chicago Cubs, was built in 1914 and is the second-oldest ballpark in the major leagues, behind Boston's Fenway Park (1912). The building, originally known as Weeghman Park, was built on grounds that were once occupied by a seminary.[15] Originally set to hold fourteen thousand seats, compared to the more than thirty-seven thousand seats it holds today, the building was estimated to cost only $250,000. During the off season, guided tours are available at Wrigley Field. Tour stops include the Cubs' dugout, the field, the visitors' clubhouse, and the W Club.[16]

Behind-the-Scenes Snapshot: Before the teams could go to Wrigley Field, they had to deliver ten Chicago-style hot dogs to fans on the roof of 3639 North Sheffield Avenue (one of the Wrigley Rooftops). My daughter, Ava, and I were sitting in the stands next to season 19 winners Ernie and Cindy as they handed out the next clue.

Address: 1060 West Addison Street, Chicago, IL 60613

Colorado | Denver

☐ Attend a Concert at Red Rocks Amphitheatre
Season 9, Episode 1, Starting Line
Episode 12, Finish Line

With an impressive seating capacity for over nine thousand people, Red Rocks Amphitheatre is a great place to attend a concert. Designated a National Historic Landmark by the National Park Service and Department of the Interior, the amphitheater is a sought-out attraction for many people across the globe.[17] With the stage uniquely surrounded by red rocks, the acoustics are perfect for any concertgoer, and the views of the surrounding area from your seat are unmatched.[18] If you don't want to attend a concert, you can also watch a film at the amphitheater, go on a hike, dine at the restaurant on the edge of the sandstone, or just fall in love with the beauty of it all.

Address: 18300 West Alameda Parkway, Morrison, CO 80465

How to get there: Fly into Denver International Airport and take the train, shuttle bus, taxi, or rent a car.

Utah | Park City

☐ *Take a Hot-Air Balloon Ride*
Season 8, Episode 10, Route Marker

At Park City High School, teams helped a pilot and crew to inflate a hot-air balloon. They then flew across the scenic Utah countryside.

The best views of Park City can be seen from above on a hot-air balloon ride. As you rise thousands of feet into the sky, you can look out upon the Kamas Valley, and gaze to the west to observe the rugged peaks of the vast Wasatch Mountains. Park City is an ideal place for hot-air ballooning because as long as the weather is tame, it can be done year-round.[19] In the winter, you might observe the snow-covered mountains, and every September a weekend is set aside to appreciate these colorful creations during Autumn Aloft, when balloonists come from all over the world to show off their special hot-air balloons.[20]

Behind-the-Scenes Snapshot: We chose this activity because Bertram and I had spent some time in New Mexico in the mid-1990s and were there for a week during the Albuquerque International Balloon Fiesta; hundreds of colorful and unique hot-air balloons filled the skies and left an indelible memory. We were able to experience hot-air ballooning again when we were scouting locations in Kenya and took a hot-air balloon safari; watching the animals roaming freely below without being disturbed by the sound of a vehicle was breathtaking. We wanted to give contestants the opportunity to experience something so special.

How to get there: Fly into Salt Lake City International Airport and take a taxi or rent a car. There are plenty of hot-air ballooning companies in the area. Feel free to choose the one you're most comfortable with.

Nevada | Las Vegas

☐ Visit the Neon Museum's "Boneyard"
Season 24, Episode 12, Route Marker

At the Neon Museum's "Boneyard" teams searched for a clue that instructed them to take a lightbulb from a silver-and-red question mark sign and bring it with them to the Mirage.

The Neon Museum was founded in 1996 and is dedicated to "collecting, preserving, and exhibiting iconic Las Vegas signs for educational, historic, arts and cultural enrichment."[21] On the grounds of the Neon Museum you can find the Neon Boneyard, which contains more than two hundred signs that are unrestored, including Las Vegas casino signs that are illuminated at sunset for viewing pleasure.[22] The museum is open seven days a week.

Address: 770 Las Vegas Boulevard North, Las Vegas, NV 89101

How to get there: Fly into McCarran International Airport and take a taxi or rent a car.

☐ *Visit Graceland Wedding Chapel*

Season 15, Episode 12, Route Marker

Teams had to travel by taxi to the Graceland Wedding Chapel and receive their next clue from The King (an Elvis Presley impersonator).

A local landmark, the Graceland Wedding Chapel is one of the oldest wedding chapels in Las Vegas and claims to be the first chapel to conduct an Elvis-themed wedding ceremony, in 1977.[23] The chapel offers traditional wedding packages as well as weddings in which an Elvis impersonator will walk the bride down the aisle and then serenade the couple by singing several Elvis hits.

Address: 619 Las Vegas Boulevard South, Las Vegas, NV 89101

> *OTHER LAS VEGAS MUST-SEES!*
>
> · *LAS VEGAS MOTOR SPEEDWAY*
> · *SALT FLATS*
> · *LAS VEGAS STRIP*
> · *THE "WELCOME TO LAS VEGAS" SIGN*
> · *HELICOPTER RIDE OVER LAS VEGAS AT NIGHT*

California | San Francisco

☐ *Take in Sweeping Views of San Francisco from the Top of Coit Tower*

Season 16, Episode 11, Roadblock

One team member had to use an ascender to reach the top archways of Coit Tower to get their next clue before being lowered back to the ground.

Coit Tower, a 210-foot concrete monument that sits at the summit of Telegraph Hill, has been an important part of the San Francisco skyline since it was constructed in 1933.[24] Upon taking an elevator to the top of the tower, views from the observation deck are 360 degrees around, allowing visitors to see the city and the bay, including the Golden Gate Bridge and the Bay Bridge.[25]

Address: 1 Telegraph Hill Boulevard, San Francisco, CA 94133

How to get there: Fly into San Francisco International Airport, then bus, taxi, drive, or take a cable car.

☐ *Take a Tour of the Golden Gate Fortune Cookie Factory*

Season 30, Episode 12, Route Marker

Teams had to properly make 102 fortune cookies, 51 per team member. Once approved, they received a giant fortune cookie to break open for their next clue.

The Golden Gate Fortune Cookie Factory, founded in 1962, is the last remaining fortune cookie factory in San Francisco. It's open seven days a week, producing up to ten thousand fortune cookies a day, and all cookies are twisted by hand by two to three employees.[26] Upon visiting the factory, you can take a tour and watch the cookies being cut into circles and folded, and you can even create your own fortune to put inside a cookie.[27]

Address: 56 Ross Alley, San Francisco, CA 94113

OTHER SAN FRANCISCO MUST-SEES!

- *GO SEE A BASEBALL GAME AT ORACLE PARK*
- *TOUR THE USS HORNET*
- *VISIT THE TONGA ROOM AT THE FAIRMONT HOTEL*
- *VISIT THE GREAT AMERICAN MUSIC HALL*

Alaska | (North of) Anchorage

☐ Ice Climb the Matanuska Glacier
Season 1, Episode 12, Roadblock

The Roadblock required one team member to climb an ice wall and retrieve their next clue from the top of the glacier.

The massive Matanuska Glacier is one hundred miles north of Anchorage and easily accessible to the public. At twenty-seven miles long and four miles wide, it's the largest glacier accessible by car in the United States. The shallow ice cliffs are suitable for introductory ice climbing, but if that isn't for you, skiing, snowshoeing, and snowmobiling are other fun options![28]

Address: Mile 102 on the Glenn Highway

How to get there: There are many tour companies offering summer and winter excursions. Fly into Ted Stevens Anchorage International Airport and rent a car.

☐ Take a Cold Dip in Fish Lake
Season 1, Episode 13, Roadblock

One team member had to strip down to their underwear or a bathing suit, plunge into the freezing waters of Fish Lake, completely submerge their head, and then retrieve their next clue.

Fish Lake is just five miles from the small mountain town of Talkeetna (which is 115 miles north of Anchorage).[29] You can take a cold dunk in the water, or if you would rather fish, you will find a variety of species in the water, including steelhead and rainbow trout.[30]

Address: Off of Talkeetna Spur Road, Talkeetna, AK 99676

How to get there: Drive from Anchorage or fly in via bush plane. There are several fishing and bush plane tour companies that conduct fish tours and overhead views if you want to experience more of what the lake has to offer.

☐ Go Dogsledding in Denali National Park
Season 1, Episode 13, Detour

Teams had to ride dogsleds eleven miles to their next clue.

A robust pack of dogs pulling a sled and a musher along a snowy trail is the ultimate Alaska adventure. Winter trips are typically November through March, depending on weather conditions, and as a rider, you can choose to ride the sled or take a turn behind the sled and mush through the snow. In summer months, you can "party on wheels," riding on the wheeled carts that the dogs use for training.[31] There are many local companies that you can contact to book this special outdoor activity.

How to get there: Fly into Fairbanks International Airport.

Alaska | Juneau

☐ Fly in a Bush Plane
Season 23, Episode 12, Roadblock

One team member flew in a bush plane in a supply drop exercise. Flying at sixty miles per hour, 150 feet above the ground, they had to drop a bag of flour from the plane and hit a target on the ground to simulate a food-and-supply drop. This is something that is done for people living and working in remote areas.

With the vast majority of Alaska inaccessible by road, bush planes are often the best mode of transportation for reaching the rugged terrain of Alaska, and they serve hundreds of remote Alaskan communities yearly.[32] Visitors can take bush plane flying tours to experience the authentic wilderness and get a glimpse of the rural life of Alaska. If you want to experience on foot the glaciers that you viewed from above, look for tours that land on the ice.[33]

Behind-the-Scenes Snapshot: Many years ago, Bertram and I filmed a pilot for a show he had just sold to Paramount called *Wild Things*. As part of filming we traveled to Sitka, Alaska, to see whales breaching, and it was my first experience in a bush plane (and what an experience it was). We always wanted to bring *The Amazing Race* to Alaska and give teams the same experience, and this Roadblock allowed us to do so!

How to get there: Fly into Juneau National Airport.

☐ *Go Sea Kayaking in the Taku Inlet*
Season 23, Episode 12, Route Marker

Teams had to paddle a tandem kayak in the Taku Inlet and search for a marked island for their next clue.

The Taku Inlet is about 7.5 miles southeast of Juneau and is excellent for kayaking, with stunning views of Taku Glacier.[34] Kayaking in Alaska is a popular way to spot wildlife such as harbor seals, sea lions, bald eagles, and occasionally a humpback whale. Numerous kayaking tours in Juneau offer views of the famous Mendenhall Glacier.[35]

How to get there: Fly or take a cruise ship into Juneau.

Hawai'i | Hawai'i Island (the "Big Island")

☐ Visit Ka Lae, the Southernmost Point in the US

Season 4, Episode 13, Roadblock

Upon arrival on the "Big Island" of Hawai'i, teams had to drive themselves to Kaulana Bay, where one team member had to swim* out to a floating tiki head, then dive to retrieve a particular rock from the ocean floor. They then carried it back to the beach and smashed it open for the clue inside.

At the end of a rugged, eleven-mile road to Kaulana Bay are the jagged, rocky cliffs of Ka Lae, the southernmost point in the United States. When you're standing on this point, there's nothing in the ocean separating you from Antarctica. It's thought that Ka Lae was the first place that Polynesians came ashore between AD 400 and 800. With ruins and sweeping views, it's no wonder that the "entire southern tip has been registered as a National Historical Landmark."[36]

Address: South Point Road, Naalehu, HI 96672

How to get there: Fly into Kona International Airport, rent a car, and drive about seventy-one miles, or fly into Hilo International Airport, rent a car, and drive about eighty miles.

---

* Because of the dangerous currents here, swimming is not recommended, but it's definitely a sight to see.

☐ *Hike Hawai'i Volcanoes National Park*
Season 4, Episode 13, Route Marker

Teams drove themselves to Hawai'i Volcanoes National Park, where they walked on a marked path over a bed of volcanic rock to get their next clue.

The park encompasses two of the world's most active volcanoes—Kilauea, which last erupted in 1984, and Mauna Loa, which last erupted in 2020. In the 523 square miles of the park, there are 150 miles of hiking trails through volcanic craters, deserts, rain forests, and petroglyphs.[37] Visit the Kilauea Visitor Center for hike suggestions and ranger-guided activities, drive along the crater rim, visit the Volcano House Hotel overlooking the Hale'mau'mau Crater, and much more!

Address: Hawai'i Volcanoes National Park, 1 Crater Rim Drive, Hawai'i National Park, HI 96718

How to get there: Fly into Hilo International Airport and rent a car. Drive about thirty-six miles to the park.

Hawai'i | Oahu Island

☐ *Skydive over Oahu*
Season 6, Episode 13, Roadblock

One team member had to tandem skydive with an instructor from eleven thousand feet, landing on a sandbar in Kaneohe Bay, to get their next clue.

Skydiving over Oahu is the perfect sightseeing opportunity, and with an added jolt of adrenaline falling through the Hawaiian skies at 120 mph it's an adventure to remember. Skydiving in Hawai'i is something that can be done year-round, so it doesn't really matter when you plan your trip.[38] There are numerous professional skydiving outlets in Hawai'i, so choose one that feels right to you.

The sandbar in Kaneohe Bay is located about a mile from the shore, so you will need a boat or kayak to get there. At low tides, the sand is exposed in the middle of the bay, perfect for beach games or setting up chairs to relax in the sun. The area is surrounded by coral reefs, perfect for snorkeling, diving, and fishing.[39]

Behind-the-Scenes Snapshot: This was a place I had been to with a friend of mine who grew up on Oahu. His family took my mother and me out on their boat, and we spent the day on the sandbar. I've always wanted to go back, and what better way than having the teams skydive right onto the sandbar?

How to get there: Fly into Oahu International Airport and rent a car.

☐ *Try Stand-up Paddle Boarding at Secret Island, Kualoa Ranch*

Season 20, Episode 12, Route Marker

Teams had to stand-up paddleboard to the finish line at Secret Island on the North Shore of Oahu.

It's widely believed that stand-up paddleboarding (also known as SUP) was invented on the island of Maui in the early 2000s. However, modern SUP is simply a revival of an already existing practice, and the history of stand-up paddling dates back thousands of years, with roots all over the globe.[40] Today, when traveling to the Hawaiian Islands, it's common to see paddleboarders along island shorelines. Of all the places to paddleboard, Hawai'i is considered one of the best.[41] If it's your first time trying paddleboarding, or if you're a pro, there are many destinations on the island with crystal-blue waters to go paddling in.

Kualoa Ranch is a four-thousand-acre private nature reserve open for guided tours. Secret Island is located within the ranch; here you can enjoy kayaking, canoe riding, stand-up paddleboarding, and beach volleyball.[42]

Address: 49-560 Kamehameha Highway, Kaneohe, HI 96744

Hawai'i | Maui Island

☐ Attend a Luau
Season 14, Episode 12, Route Marker

Teams had to season a 145-pound pig with island flavoring and carry it suspended on a bamboo pole two hundred yards along the beach to a Hawaiian luau. At the luau, they had to properly cover the pig for a traditional kalua cooking.

The first feast/luau is thought to have been held around 1819. A Hawaiian luau, a feast featuring music and vibrant cultural performances from greater Polynesia and Hawai'i, is one of the best ways to experience Hawaiian culture.[43] Each Hawaiian island has several luaus to choose from, "ranging from kitschy to chic," and each with different cuisine options, so find one that suits you![44]

How to get there: Maui has three airports: Kahului Airport, Kapalua Airport, and Hana Airport. From there you can rent a car or take a taxi to the place you've booked.

Canada

Calgary

☐ Mountain Bike at Canada Olympic Park

Season 5, Episode 13, Detour

Teams used mountain bikes to ride a snow-covered slalom ski course down the Olympic ski slope and had to complete the course in three minutes or less to receive their next clue.

Calgary hosted the 1988 Winter Olympic Games, leaving behind a park full of multi-season activities. During the summer months, you can take a chairlift up to fourteen mountain bike trails.[45] Additionally, there are also mountain biking camps for children of all ages and skill levels. Other available winter activities include skiing, snowboarding, bobsled, hockey, tubing, and skating.[46]

Address: 88 Canada Olympic Road SW, Calgary, Alberta T3B 5R5, Canada

How to get there: Fly into Calgary International Airport and rent a car or take a taxi or bus.

☐ *Hike to the Continental Divide*

Season 5, Episode 13, Route Marker

Inside Banff National Park (at Banff Sunshine Village), teams had to take a gondola to the base of Lookout Mountain. Next, teams put on snowshoes and hiked one thousand feet up to the top ridge of the Continental Divide to find their next clue.

Banff is Canada's first national park and is home to three ski resorts: Banff Sunshine Village, Lake Louise, and Mount Norquay. Banff Sunshine Village is located at an altitude of 7,082 feet, straddling the Continental Divide in the heart of the Canadian Rockies.[47] Sunshine Village's three mountains—Lookout Mountain, Mount Standish, and Goat's Eye Mountain—offer vast terrain to ski. Guided snowshoe trekking tours that cross the Continental Divide are available at Banff Sunshine Village through the White Mountain Adventures company.[48]

Address: Banff Sunshine Village, 1 Sunshine Access Road, Banff, Alberta T1L 1J5, Canada

Toronto

☐ *Take a Cruise in the Toronto Harbor on the Kajama Schooner*

Season 8, Episode 11, Detour

Teams sailed across Toronto Harbor from Queens Quay to the schooner *Kajama*. One team member had to climb one hundred feet to the top of the mast to retrieve a nautical flag to receive their next clue.

The *Kajama* is a traditional 165-foot three-masted schooner that sets sail daily from May to September in the Toronto Harbor. You can take a two-hour-long day or sunset cruise on the open waters of Lake Ontario, either sitting back and relaxing or assisting the crew to get the full sailing experience. On each trip, the crew fires off the ship's cannon.[49]

Address: 235 Queens Quay West, Toronto, Ontario M5J 2B8, Canada

How to get there: Fly into Toronto Pearson International Airport and take a train, bus, or car.

☐ *Go to the Top of the CN Tower*
Season 8, Episode 11, Route Marker

At the CN Tower, teams took an elevator to the observation deck at 1,122 feet. They then used binoculars to look for the next clue marker at Polson Pier.

The CN Tower defines Toronto's skyline at a whopping 1,815 feet. Following completion of construction on the tower in 1976, the building held the record for the world's tallest freestanding structure for thirty-two years. The antenna makes it the tallest tower in the western hemisphere. Each year, more than 1.5 million people visit the CN Tower, a tower that is not only a beautiful addition to the skyline but one that solves communication problems and provides clear transmission to Toronto's residents.[50]

Address: 290 Bremner Boulevard, Toronto, Ontario M5V 3L9, Canada

Montréal

☐ Fly on the Trapeze
at Le Château de Cirque
Season 8, Episode 11, Roadblock

At Trapezium, one team member had to successfully complete a flying trapeze maneuver known as a "catch," where they had to swing from the platform, turn upside down, hang from their legs, and then reach out midair to the trapeze artist on the other swing, who would catch them so they could receive their next clue.

Trapezium, also known as Le Château de Cirque, offers many unique circus classes adapted to all levels. These include flying trapeze, rope, lyra, silk, Chinese pole, static trapeze, flexibility, and hand to hand.[51] No circus background is necessary.

Behind-the-Scenes Snapshot: In the mid-1990s, my parents took me to my first Cirque du Soleil show in New York City, and I've been a fan ever since. Seeing many of their shows in Los Angeles and Las Vegas, I was inspired to have a circus performance challenge in The Amazing Race. Since Cirque du Soleil was founded in Canada, it was the perfect place for this task.

Address: 6956 Saint Denis Street, Montréal, Quebec H2S 2S4, Canada

How to get there: Fly into Montréal-Pierre Elliott Trudeau International Airport and then drive or take the metro.

☐ *Visit the Montréal Biosphère Museum*
Season 8, Episode 11, Route Marker

At the Montréal Biosphère, teams had to climb the stairs to the fifth floor and get their next clue.

The Biosphère in Montréal is the only museum in North America wholly dedicated to the environment and aims to raise awareness on environmental issues plaguing North America and the world.[52] Designed by American architect Buckminster Fuller for the Expo 67 world's fair, the height of the geodesic dome is comparable to a twenty-story building.[53] The Biosphère is open to the public and has an observation deck on the fifth floor.

Address: 160 Chemin du Tour-de-l'Isle, Île Sainte-Hélène, Montréal H3C 4G8, Canada

SOUTH AMERICA

Brazil

Rio de Janeiro

☐ *Go to the Top of Sugarloaf Mountain*
Season 2, Episode 1, Detour

Teams had to rappel 590 feet down the face of Sugarloaf Mountain to receive their next clue.

At its peak of 1,296 feet, Sugarloaf Mountain offers panoramic views of Guanabara Bay and the city of Rio. You can take a cable car up to the top to appreciate the views, or if you would rather hike, it's possible to walk up Morro da Urca, which is halfway up. From there, you can purchase a ticket for a cable car to take you the rest of the way. Hiking up the first half is relatively easy, lasting about twenty-five minutes through the jungle. If you're feeling truly adventurous, you can climb all the way to the top, but that is only recommended for those with substantial rock-climbing experience who have their own gear, and who have hired an experienced guide to help climb the challenging trails that lead up the mountain.[1] In accordance with the Conservation Authority of Sugarloaf, rappelling is currently forbidden on Sugarloaf Mountain, but it's definitely worth the visit for the views alone.[2]

Address: Avenue Pasteur, 520, Urca, Rio de Janeiro, RJ 22290-240, Brazil

How to get there: Fly into Rio de Janeiro/Galeão International Airport and take a taxi, bus, or rent a car.

☐ *Visit Christ the Redeemer*
Season 2, Episode 1, Route Marker

Upon arriving in Rio de Janeiro, teams had to travel to the Christ the Redeemer statue on Corcovado Mountain to find their next clue.

Completed in 1931 and standing at the summit of the 2,300-foot Corcovado Mountain is the famous statue of Jesus. Coming in at ninety-eight feet tall, the statue has a wingspan of ninety-two feet and is the largest Art Deco–style statue in the world. The statue is thought to be representative of the nation of Brazil and the city of Rio de Janeiro as a whole, and is considered one of the new Seven Wonders of the World.[3] The most interesting and exciting way to travel to the statue is by cog train, but make sure you purchase tickets in advance to avoid waiting in line! If you're feeling adventurous, you can hike up the mountain, or if need be, you can also take a taxi or car to the peak.[4]

Address: Parque Nacional da Tijuca, Alto da Boa Vista, Rio de Janeiro, RJ, Brazil

☐ *Take a Helicopter Tour over Rio de Janeiro*
Season 27, Episode 1, Route Marker

From the heliport in Lagoa, teams flew in a helicopter past Christ the Redeemer and, once they landed, they had to identify and recite the statue's name to the helicopter pilot before receiving their next clue.

If you want to see Christ the Redeemer from above (in addition to many other beautiful Rio sights), a helicopter tour may be the best way to do so. There are many companies that offer these tours, so choose one that feels good to you and offers you the sights and duration you're looking for.

Heliport Address: Av. Borges de Medeiros, 1892–1932, Lagoa, Rio de Janeiro, RJ, Brazil

☐ Visit the Carioca Aqueduct and Walk Along the Famous Escadaria Selarón

Season 18, Episode 11, Route Marker

Teams had to take a tram up to the top of the Carioca Aqueduct and then travel on foot to Escadaria Selarón. There, they had to search the tile-covered steps for an Amazing Race tile that had their next clue on the back.

The Carioca Aqueduct, located in the city center of Rio, was built in the eighteenth century to bring fresh water into the city. In the nineteenth century, the aqueduct was adapted to serve as a bridge for the tram connecting the city center to the hilly Santa Teresa neighborhood. You can take the tram and appreciate the views of the famous Escadaria Selarón before traveling there to walk along the steps.[5]

One of Rio's most-loved attractions, the Selarón Steps (Escadaria Selarón) became a work of art when Chilean-born artist Jorge Selarón covered them with colorful mosaic tiles as a dedication to the Brazilian people. The 215 steps are covered in over two thousand tiles, many locally sourced and many donated by visitors from over sixty countries around the world.[6] It's free to visit the Selarón Steps, and make sure you bring a camera!

Aqueduct Address: Rua Riachuelo 27, Rio de Janeiro, RJ 20230-010, Brazil

Escadaria Selarón Address: R. Manuel Carneiro, Santa Teresa, Rio de Janeiro, RJ 20241-120, Brazil

☐ Hang Glide from the Top of Pedra Bonita Mountain

Season 27, Episode 1, Fast Forward

In the season's only Fast Forward, each team had to tandem hang glide from seventeen hundred feet at the Pedra Bonita Ramp (located in Tijuca Forest National Park) to São Conrado Pepino Beach to win the Fast Forward award.

With a height of 2,283 feet, Pedra Bonita is perfect for hiking, paragliding, or hang gliding. Here, at one of the hidden treasures of Rio, you can choose to simply hike up and down the mountain, or you can choose to hike up and soar down over the stunning scenery, experiencing the unique jungle-meets-city landscape below, and landing on the white sands of São Conrado Pepino Beach.[7] There are many hang gliding companies that offer packages, so make sure to pick one that you feel comfortable with and enjoy the spectacular views!

Behind-the-Scenes Snapshot: While scouting this location, I had to put myself in the contestants' shoes and hang glide off the mountain. It was my first time tandem hang gliding, and I was petrified. I was on the top of the mountain, standing on a wooden ramp that sloped downward, and I was told to run as fast as I could down the ramp and off into thin air! I did, and it was amazing; I soared through the air like a bird, and eventually landed on the white sandy beach below. I knew the minute after we took off that we had to add this activity to the next season of *The Amazing Race*.

> OTHER RIO MUST-SEES!
>
> • COPACABANA BEACH
> • IPANEMA BEACH
> • JARDIM BOTÂNICO
>   (BOTANICAL GARDEN)
> • TEATRO MUNICIPAL

Address: Estrada da Cascatinha, 850, Alto da Boa Vista, Rio de Janeiro, RJ 20531-590, Brazil

Manaus

☐ *Shop at Mercado Municipal Adolpho Lisboa*

Season 32, Episode 3, Route Marker

Teams had to purchase items from a list written in Portuguese (cassava root, a tipiti, two pairs of gloves, tucupi, two hammocks, tucumã peelings, a steel machete, cassava flour, ten hot peppers, pirarucu, and a thermal bag) and then bring them to the dock manager at Balsa Laranja to receive their next clue.

Built in 1882, the Manaus historic city market is a downsized replica of the Les Halles market in Paris. Bustling with culture and excitement, the market contains handicraft shops, a working fish market, and many great places to eat throughout.[8] It's truly a sight to be seen. "With its soaring tin roof and stained-glass windows, the century-old Manaus fish market is nothing if not a temple dedicated to Amazonian biodiversity, a museum of the soon-to-be-eaten, illuminated by strings of hanging 15-watt bulbs."[9]

Address: 46 Rua dos Barés, Manaus, Brazil

How to get there: Fly into Manaus International Airport—Eduardo Gomes and take a taxi.

Argentina

Buenos Aires

☐ Visit the Grave of Evita Perón
Season 5, Episode 2, Route Marker

Upon arrival in Buenos Aires, teams had to find the grave of former Argentine first lady Evita Perón (which they had to figure out was at La Recoleta Cemetery) to get their next clue.

The Duarte family crypt at La Recoleta Cemetery is the final resting place of Eva Perón (Evita). Evita was the second wife of Argentine Juan Perón, and although she never held a government job, she acted as a "de facto minister of health and labor, awarding generous wage increases to the unions, who responded with political support for Perón."[10] Located in the neighborhood of Recoleta, the cemetery is unlike any other in the world. Make sure to grab a map at the entrance, because this is certainly an easy place to get lost, with no fewer than 6,400 graves. Each grave is unique, with nods to different styles of architecture, such as Art Deco, Neo-Gothic, Baroque, and more. With many important Argentinians buried here, the fourteen-acre site is a must when visiting Buenos Aires.[11]

Address: Junín 1760, C1113 CABA, Argentina

How to get there: Fly into Ministro Pistarini International Airport, Ezeiza, then take a taxi, bus, or rent a car.

☐ *Learn to Tango*

Season 27, Episode 2, Roadblock

At Aerea Teatro, one team member had to learn and properly perform a tango routine, which included a second half where they were harnessed and had to finish the steps on the wall of a stage, to receive their next clue.

Such a vital part of the Buenos Aires experience, tango originated toward the end of the nineteenth century and was first danced by working-class men (at the time, it was obscene to think that women could dance with men, so men danced together instead).[12] As a visitor, you can start with a private lesson; your hotel can put you in contact with a school, or you can do some research on your own to decide what you're looking to get out of the experience. If dancing is not for you but you want to feel a part of the tango culture, attend a tango show for a fun night out.

Address: Bartolomé Mitre 4272, C1201 ABD, Buenos Aires, Argentina

☐ *Watch a Live Polo Match*

Season 27, Episode 2, Pit Stop

After completing the Roadblock, teams were told to go to "the Cathedral of Polo," leaving them to figure out it referred to the Campo Argentino de Polo.

Built in 1928, this venue hosts many, if not all, important polo matches in the country, including the Argentine Polo Tournament. Other big events are held at the venue as well, and with the stadium holding more than thirty thousand people, it's easy to do. While most of the time official matches are ticketed and must be paid for, you can sometimes see local polo clubs play at the stadium for free.[13]

Address: Avenue del Libertador 4096, C1426 CABA, Argentina

☐ *Indulge in Chocolate at Del Turista Chocolate Factory*

Season 5, Episode 3, Roadblock

At Del Turista Chocolate Factory one team member had to search through eleven thousand chocolates by biting into them until they found one of only twenty with a white center to receive their next clue.

The Patagonian city of Bariloche is especially known for chocolate. With many different chocolatiers throughout the city, this town follows in the footsteps of its European forefathers when it comes to passion behind everything chocolate.[14] The Del Turista Chocolate Factory is specifically rooted in the Swiss-Italian traditions when it comes to chocolate making and has remained a part of the same family-run business since 1969. Their shop is one of the most popular among the competing companies in Bariloche, with their master chocolatiers making more than two hundred varieties of chocolate.[15]

Address: 239 Mitre, Centro, San Carlos de Bariloche, Rio Negro, Argentina

San Antonio de Areco

☐ *Live like a Gaucho*

Season 27, Episode 3, Roadblock

At Estancia la Porteña de Areco, one member had to properly prepare a traditional *asado* meal by skewering and hanging two racks of lamb and one rack of beef ribs onto a set of metal grills to receive their next clue.

Grilled meat in Argentina is an art form and part of what makes Argentina so special. Traditional *asado* is associated with the idea of the gaucho, dating back to a time when gauchos, or cowboys, roamed the Pampas and were able to survive on the meat of their stock.[16] Because it dates back so far, it's as simple as can be: fire, grill, and meat. Borrowing from the gaucho's need to use all elements of the stock, an *asado* includes different parts of the animal, not just the good pieces of meat.[17] You can visit Estancia la Porteña de Areco and take part in the real gaucho experience. Tours include caring for horses, farming, and a traditional gaucho lunch.

Behind-the-Scenes Snapshot: The first time I visited Argentina, I attempted to go to dinner around 6:30 p.m., and nothing was open. I had no idea that the locals don't even think about eating dinner before 9:00 p.m.!

Address: Km N 110 Ruta Nacional 8, San Antonio de Areco 2760, Argentina

How to get there: Fly into San Carlos de Bariloche Airport and take a taxi or a bus, or rent a car.

Chile

Iquique

☐ ***Paraglide from Alto Hospicio to the Beach***

Season 23, Episode 1, Roadblock

One team member had to direct their taxi to follow their partner, who was paragliding from Alto Hospicio down to Playa Brava or Playa Huayquique. Once team members reunited on the beach, the glide master gave them their next clue.

The port town of Iquique in northern Chile is one of the best locations in the world to go paragliding. Averaging only seven non-flyable days per year, the Atacama Desert is a paragliding wonder; taking off from the high cliffs of Alto Hospicio, you will take in the unique and beautiful view of the city where the desert meets the ocean.[18] There are many companies that offer paragliding in Iquique, with different itineraries and jumping-off points, so find the one that is the most interesting to you!

Takeoff Address: Circunvalación 3212, Alto Hospicio, Tarapacá, Chile

Landing Address: Playa Brava Beach or Huayquique Beach, Iquique, Tarapacá, Chile

How to get there: Fly into Diego Aracena International Airport and take a taxi or rent a car.

(Southeast of) Santiago

☐ Zip-Line at Cascada de las Ánimas
Season 23, Episode 2, Pit Stop

Some teams rode the zip line at Cascada de las Ánimas before checking into the Pit Stop. Once it was nighttime, teams could no longer ride the zip line and simply checked in. In addition, the Pit Stop mat was moved off the suspension bridge once it was nighttime.

The zip line over the Maipo River at Cascada de las Ánimas allows you to soar over pine and eucalyptus trees and experience the wonderful feeling of flying while enjoying views of the snowy Andean summits and the Maipo River. One of the longest zip line rides in Chile, the cables are suspended 80 feet above the river and stretch over 558 feet across the canyon. With speeds up to 31 mph, you're sure to enjoy this amazing, once-in-a-lifetime ride.[19]

Address: Camino al Volcán 31087, Casilla 57, San Alfonso, San José de Maipo, Región Metropolitana, Chile

How to get there: Fly into Comodoro Arturo Merino Benítez International Airport and take a bus, taxi, or rent a car.

> OTHER SANTIAGO MUST-SEES!
>
> - TAKE A RIDE ON THE FUNICULAR RAILWAY ASCENSOR ARTILLERIA
> - VISIT PALACIO BABURIZZA
> - VISIT PABLO NERUDA'S HOME, LA SEBASTIANA

EUROPE

Paris

☐ **Walk the Underground Sewers of Paris**

Season 1, Episode 3, Roadblock

One team member had to suit up in front of the Hôtel de Ville and enter the underground sewers to search for their next clue before exiting aboveground at Place du Châtelet.

Baron Haussmann and engineer Eugène Belgrand designed the modern Paris sewer system in the year 1850. Less than thirty years later, the system was over 373 miles long, and today it extends farther than the route from New York to Miami, at 1,304 miles long (and this is all beneath the streets of Paris!).[1] The sewers below almost mirror the traditional streets above them, and the space is big enough to accommodate one person. If you chose to, you could walk the entirety of Paris underground (especially because there are street signs down there too!). Visit the Paris Sewer Museum (Musée des égouts de Paris) and take a self-guided tour.

Behind-the-Scenes Snapshot: Paris has a special place in my heart. I first visited the city on my backpacking trip after graduating from college. I remember the train arriving at Gare du Nord and how excited I was to set foot in the city. I had studied French in school and had been practicing by writing letters to a friend in Paris whom I'd met in New York City. When Bertram and I were creating the route for season 1, I knew Paris was one of the places I wanted to bring the contestants to; there's something so magical about it.

Museum Address: Musée des égouts de Paris, Pont de l'Alma— Face au 93 quai d'Orsay, 75007 Paris, France

Hotel Address: Hôtel de Ville, Place de l'Hôtel de Ville, 75004 Paris, France

How to get there: Fly into Paris Charles de Gaulle Airport, then take the metro, a bus or taxi, or rent a car. Alternatively you can also fly into Orly Airport and take a bus or rent a car.

☐ *Climb to the Top of the Sacré-Cœur Basilica*
Season 27, Episode 6, Route Marker

At Square Louise-Michel in front of the Sacré-Cœur Basilica, teams had to search the grounds for *Le Fantôme Blanc*, who handed them their next clue.

This nineteenth-century basilica is one of Paris's most famous landmarks (and rightfully so). Since 1885, this site has been a place for prayers for humanity and peace. Because this is a sacred site, make sure you're dressed modestly and conduct yourself in a mature manner. Inspired by churches in Turkey and Italy, the white stone on the exterior was chosen for its self-cleaning capabilities: "when it rains, it secretes a chalky substance that acts as a fresh coat of paint."[2] The exterior is lovely, but the interiors of this basilica are something else. The ceiling features a gorgeous mosaic pattern that was installed in the 1920s, and the belfry houses five beautiful bells, one of which is the largest in France (weighing a massive twenty-one tons!).[3] You can visit the basilica and simply enjoy the exterior and interior features, or you can take it one step further and climb the three hundred stairs to the top of the dome (which also happens to be the second-highest point in Paris). The panoramic views of the city are unmatched.

Address: 35 Rue du Chevalier de la Barre, 75018 Paris, France

☐ *Enjoy the Royal Platter at La Coupole*
Season 27, Episode 6, Detour

Teams traveled to La Coupole Brasserie to make its signature dish, the Royal Platter. The dish consists of crab, lobster, langoustines, prawns, and eighteen oysters. If they reached the chef's high standard of presentation, they received their next clue.

Established in 1927, during the Roaring Twenties, La Coupole is the largest brasserie in Paris. The Art Deco interior is the same as it was when famous artists and authors such as Hemingway and Picasso visited the restaurant, and the thirty-three painted columns found throughout the space were painted by twenty-seven famous artists of the time. The menu focuses on traditional French cuisine with a spotlight on fresh shellfish.[4]

Address: 102 Boulevard du Montparnasse, 75014 Paris, France

> OTHER PARIS MUST-SEES!
>
> · EIFFEL TOWER
> · ARC DE TRIOMPHE
> · CHAMPS-ÉLYSÉES
> · THE LOUVRE MUSEUM
> · MOULIN ROUGE
> · PONT ALEXANDRE III
> · CATACOMBS OF PARIS
> · BATEAUX MOUCHES
> · CHÂTEAU DE CHANTILLY
> · NOTRE-DAME CATHEDRAL

Chamonix

☐ Place du Triangle de l'Amitié
Season 28, Episode 4, Pit Stop

After the Roadblock in Geneva, Switzerland, teams were told to travel by train to Chamonix, France, and search for the Pit Stop at Place du Triangle de l'Amitié.

Known as the Triangle of Friendship, the town square (actually in the shape of a triangle) in Chamonix celebrates the peaceful collaboration of Italy, Switzerland, and France, with all three countries actually touching in this area.[5] An internationally known mountain resort in the French Alps, Chamonix-Mont-Blanc is considered a world capital for winter sports. In fact, they hosted the first Winter Olympic Games in 1924! At an elevation of 3,402 feet, Mont Blanc can be climbed from Chamonix, or you can take a cable car from the town center up to Aiguille du Midi (where most people start their hike).[6] Keep in mind that this hike is for more experienced climbers that have the proper gear and a guide to assist.

Address: Aiguille du Midi cable car, 100 Place de l'Aiguille du Midi, 74400 Chamonix-Mont-Blanc, France

How to get there: Fly into Geneva Airport in Switzerland and take a train or rent a car.

☐ Paraglide Above Chamonix
Season 28, Episode 5, Roadblock

The leg's Roadblock required one team member to take the Brévent Cable Car and ascend to Planpraz. They would then take a running jump and tandem paraglide several thousand feet off the side of the Aiguilles Rouges. Racers were only permitted to run one at a time, and if they failed to take off, they would have to try again. Once in the air, they had to spot a yeti waving a French flag. And once they landed, they had to correctly identify the flag they'd seen (France) to receive their next clue.

Chamonix is a great place to paraglide if you have never done it before! It's known as *parapenting* in France, and there are many instructors and companies in the area that will safely get you up into the sky.[7] The instructor will maneuver the parachute and do all the hard work while you take in the view of Chamonix from above. All flight schools in Chamonix have strict safety standards, so pick a company that sits right with you and soar!

Address: Brévent Cable Car, 29 Route Henriette d'Angeville, 74400 Chamonix-Mont-Blanc, France

Saint-Tropez

☐ Take Sailing Lessons
Season 30, Episode 4, Roadblock

One team member had to attach a sail to an Optimist sailing dinghy and then sail across the bay without being given any prior lessons, to two buoys, each holding one-half of their next clue. Once they retrieved the two clue halves, they had to sail to the shore and reunite with their partner before opening their clue.

Along its famous Pampelonne Beach, the village resort of Saint-Tropez offers amazing water activities, including wakeboarding, Jet Skiing, parasailing, paddleboarding, snorkeling, diving, and even flyboarding![8] Saint-Tropez is also well known for the super-yachts that fill its harbor for the famous Voiles de Saint-Tropez regatta every year. If you're interested in learning to sail, there are several sailing schools in the Saint-Tropez area that offer lessons for children and adults.

Address: Pampelonne Beach, Route des Plages Plusieurs accès depuis la route des plages, 83350 Ramatuelle, Saint-Tropez, France

How to get there: You can fly into Nice Airport, which is about thirty-nine miles away. At the airport you can rent a car or take a bus or train.

United Kingdom | England

London

☐ *Ride the London Eye*
Season 7, Episode 10, Route Marker

At the London Eye, teams had to board a capsule and survey the city to locate a Route Marker and their next clue, which was at the London Marriott Hotel County Hall.

The London Eye is not a Ferris wheel, but instead is the world's tallest cantilevered observation wheel. At an overall height of 443 feet, it takes thirty minutes to make one revolution and moves at a rate slow enough that it never has to stop to let passengers on and off. Each of the thirty-two "capsules" corresponds to one of the thirty-two boroughs that make up Greater London, and each can hold twenty-five passengers.[9] The Eye was originally designed as a temporary structure (with the ability to dismantle the wheel and move it to different cities), but it was so popular that it was made a permanent London fixture.[10]

Address: Riverside Building, County Hall, South Bank, London SE1 7PB, United Kingdom

How to get there: Fly into Heathrow Airport and take a taxi, train, bus, or rent a car.

☐ *Visit the Tower Bridge*

Season 25, Episode 2, Detour

Once in London, teams had to head to the Tower Bridge and search for the Pearly King and Queen, who gave them their next clue.

The Tower Bridge is one of London's most famous landmarks. The bridge was completed in 1894, and it had taken eight years and the relentless labor of 432 workers to complete.[11] The twin towers reach a height of two hundred feet over the Thames, and between the towers is a pair of glass-covered walkways. Until 1976, the bridge was operated by hydraulic pumps driven by steam, but now it's operated by electric motors. The original power system is still kept in good condition and is on display for tourists to see. Because shipping has decreased at the London Docklands, the bridge is rarely lifted to allow boats and barges to pass through.[12]

Address: Tower Bridge Road, London SE1 2UP, United Kingdom

☐ *Go Boating on the Serpentine in Hyde Park*

Season 31, Episode 11, Detour

Teams had to row a double scull through a 660-foot course on the Serpentine in Hyde Park in under one minute to receive their next clue.

Hyde Park was created by Henry VIII in 1536 and is the largest Royal Park in Central London; the Queen specifically was the one to ask for the man-made lake, the Serpentine. Other countries across the globe took note of its natural design, and not too long after, other man-made lakes started popping up all over the place! Both rowing and pedal boats are available for rent on the forty-acre Serpentine; make sure to remember while you're paddling that, like most parts of London, the Serpentine is rich in history and tradition.[13] You can also take a ride on the SolarShuttle, which glides silently across the lake powered only by the sun. Boating on the Serpentine is open from April until October.

Address: London W2 2UH, England

☐ *Explore Iconic Camden Market*
Season 31, Episode 11, Pit Stop

At Camden Market, teams found the Pit Stop and host Phil Keoghan, who surprised them with a clue. Teams had to search Camden Market for the items in a display and, once they found the items, arrange them to re-create the same display before they could check in at the Pit Stop.

Open since 1974, Camden Market has over a thousand places to shop, eat, drink, and dance in its historic central London location. Camden Market started off with sixteen stalls, as a small arts and crafts fair. Originally it was only open on Sundays; however, its popularity grew fast. Today it's the largest market in London, open seven days a week. It's the most concentrated place in London to search for original and unusual merchandise from hundreds of independent shops.[14]

Address: 54–56 Camden Lock Place, Camden Town, London NW1 8AF, United Kingdom

Behind-the-Scenes Snapshot: I remember the moment vividly: I was watching Claire attempt the Roadblock, which was supposed to be fun: put a watermelon into a giant slingshot and hit a target (a suit of armor) not too far away. Simple enough, right? Not really. Claire pulled back so hard on the slingshot that the band holding the watermelon flipped around, sending the watermelon torpedoing right into her face! When the shocking moment happened, several of us (including our medic) immediately ran to Claire. We were afraid of what we might find, as it appeared that she might be badly injured given how hard the watermelon had hit her. The watermelon had exploded into pieces; what was her face going to look like? Miraculously, she was okay, but she had a severe headache and numbness in her cheek for days! How incredible that she was all right and continued on. Strong woman!

OTHER UNITED KINGDOM MUST-SEES!

- *VISIT SOMERSET HOUSE*
- *VISIT VICTORIA TOWER GARDENS*
- *ATTEND THE CHANGING OF THE GUARD*
- *VISIT STONEHENGE IN AMESBURY*
- *VISIT EASTNOR CASTLE, THE SITE OF THE INFAMOUS ROADBLOCK WHERE CLAIRE WAS HIT IN THE FACE WITH A WATERMELON THAT BACKFIRED IN SEASON 17, EPISODE 1*

Cambridge

☐ Learn How to Punt

Season 3, Episode 3, Detour

In this Detour, teams rowed a local boat called a punt with only a long pole and a small paddle to navigate one mile down the River Cam.

A punt is a square-ended, long, flat-bottom boat. Punts are usually propelled by using a long pole (which is also used to steer). The boats were developed in medieval times to allow navigation into shallow waters in areas where traditional boats could not go.[15] Punting is the most popular form of boating on the stretch of the River Cam between Jesus Lock and Grantchester. Several companies in Cambridge offer punting lessons.

Address: La Mimosa Punt Station, Thompson's Lane, Cambridge CB5 8AQ, United Kingdom

How to get there: From Heathrow Airport, take a taxi, train, or rent a car.

☐ *Ride the Underground Mail Rail*
Season 33, Episode 2, Roadblock

One team member had to ride an underground train along the Mail Rail to a loading dock and sort through a bin filled with packages and envelopes to find their next clue.

The Mail Rail, also known as the Post Office Railway, was a railway that once ran close to nineteen hours a day, seventy feet below the surface. For over seventy-five years, from 1927 to 2003, the Mail Rail was used to move close to four million letters a day across London.[16] If you visit the Postal Museum, you can ride the underground Mail Rail and learn all about how letters got around London for so many years.

Museum Address: 15–20 Phoenix Place, London WC1X 0DL, United Kingdom

Reykjavík

☐ ***Swim in the Blue Lagoon***
Season 6, Episode 1, Pit Stop

The Blue Lagoon is the most popular tourist attraction in Iceland, bringing around 360,000 visitors a year (this is 20 percent more than the entire population of Iceland!). The blue-green water is a warm 100°F, and features mineral salts and fine silica mud, both of which exfoliate and soften the skin naturally.[17] The lagoon is surrounded by black lava rocks, which make for a relaxing and otherworldly environment.

Address: Norðurljósavegur 9, 240 Grindavík, Iceland

How to get there: Fly into Keflavík Airport and take a taxi or rent a car.

☐ ***Visit the Seljalandsfoss Waterfall***
Season 6, Episode 1, Route Marker

Once in Iceland, teams picked up a marked car with their next clue in it, instructing them to drive to the Seljalandsfoss waterfall to retrieve their next clue.

Seljalandsfoss is unique, one of the most special waterfalls in Iceland because you can walk behind its 196-foot cascade (and maybe even catch a rainbow in the water spray on a sunny day!). Iceland is said to be home to ten thousand waterfalls, some more popular, like Gullfoss on the Golden Circle in Northern Iceland and Skógafoss in Southern Iceland.[18]

☐ *Ride Snowmobiles on a Glacier*
Season 6, Episode 1, Route Marker

At the base of Vatnajökull glacier, teams had to sign up for a shuttle bus to take them ten miles to the glacier's edge for their next clue. Once at the glacier's edge, teams chose a marked snowmobile and drove across the glacier to a camp.

Vatnajökull glacier began forming twenty-five hundred years ago and is the largest glacier in Europe. Covering more than 8 percent of the country, the ice has an average thickness of twelve hundred feet.[19] Vatnajökull National Park (along with the glacier) covers 14 percent of Iceland, and there are several professional tour companies that offer guided snowmobile excursions and tours to see the ice caves.

Behind-the-Scenes Snapshot: Sometimes the ideas we come up with sound fun and entertaining until we actually test them out. I had an idea to put the contestants on skis and pull them behind a snowmobile, and a glacier in Iceland sounded like the perfect place to test this out. Well, the test was fun for about thirty seconds and then it just felt much too dangerous. To do the task safely, the snowmobile would have to go very slow, so we decided to have the contestants snowmobile across the glacier instead, which turned out to be super exciting and quite an adrenaline rush!

Address: Vatnajökull National Park, Urridaholtsstraeti 6-8, 210 Gardabaer, Iceland

Oslo

☐ *Zip-Line down the World-Famous Holmenkollen Ski Jump*

Season 6, Episode 2, Roadblock

One team member had to climb to the top of the ski jump, then ride a zip line one thousand feet to the bottom to receive the next clue.

Holmenkollen ski jump in Oslo is one of Norway's most visited attractions. The ski jump itself has been rebuilt nineteen times since it was first constructed in 1892, because it's so popular and gets so much foot traffic![20] The last time it was rebuilt was 2010, and it now weighs one thousand tons and is made of steel.

Something special about this attraction is that this zip line was originally conceived by the *Amazing Race* team for the Roadblock in 2004! Flying down the 1,184-foot zip line with an elevation drop of 352 feet, you will feel an intense rush of adrenaline! Holmenkollen is open to the public in the spring, summer, and fall. The ticket includes entry to the Ski Museum as well. If you're afraid of heights and don't want to ride the actual zip line, you can also find how it feels to fly down the ski jump using their new ski simulator.

Behind-the-Scenes Snapshot: I was excited to take the teams to Norway, as there was a giant ski jump in Oslo and we had the idea to create a zip line from the top of the jump all the way to the bottom. We wanted to give the contestants the same feeling Olympic ski jumpers get as they soar through the sky. We brought our rigging company over to

Norway to see if it was possible, and it was! They created an amazing zip line, and after we finished filming, the company that runs the ski jump built their own zip line. It's become a very popular tourist attraction.

Address: Kongeveien 5, 0787 Oslo, Norway

How to get there: Fly into Oslo Airport Gardermoen and take a taxi, train, bus, or rent a car.

Narvik

☐ *Ride the Cable Car up Fagernesfjellet Mountain*
Season 17, Episode 5, Route Marker

Upon arrival in Narvik, teams had to find Fagernesfjellet mountain, and then ride the Narvikfjellet cable car to the top of the mountain to retrieve their next clue.

Refurbished in 1995 and only half a mile from the town center is this modern cable car that takes you to the summit of Fagernesfjellet mountain. The ride lasts only seven minutes, and takes you over two thousand feet up to the top, where you can eat at the peak restaurant or follow slopes down to the water's edge.[21] You're likely to see hang gliders and paragliders soaring around the mountainside. Recently, snowboarding has become very popular in Narvik (in addition to the already popular skiing), and the mountain is open for these winter sports from October/ November through May. The mountain is also open in the summer, for hiking and other activities.

Address: Skistuaveien 57, 8515 Narvik, Norway

How to get there: Fly into Oslo Airport Gardermoen, then transfer to Harstad-Narvik Airport and from there take a taxi or rent a car.

Amsterdam

☐ ## Take a "HotTug" through the City's Canals

Season 26, Episode 9, Detour

Teams had to pilot an electric-powered hot tub called a HotTug through the city's canals, while solving a rebus puzzle along the route. Once teams wrote down the right answer, they received their next clue.

Developed in 2012, a HotTug is a wood-fired sailing hot tub. The electrically propelled boat can seat up to six people comfortably, with the water temperature set to a steamy one hundred degrees. Because of the water temperature, the tub can be enjoyed year-round! The team took their ride in Amsterdam, but you can experience a HotTug in other cities as well, including Rotterdam, Helsinki, London, and Zurich.[22]

Address: Wijnhaven 101, 3011 WN Rotterdam, Netherlands

How to get there: Fly into Amsterdam Airport Schiphol and take a taxi, train, or rent a car.

☐ ## Ride a Bicycle Around Amsterdam

Season 26, Episode 9, Route Marker

After the Roadblock, teams had to ride bicycles along the Amstel River to the historic Munttoren tower in Amsterdam to find their next clue.

With more than three hundred miles of dedicated bike paths and lanes, Amsterdam is best seen by cycling. With a population of 17 million, the Dutch own 22.5 million bicycles (there are more bikes than people!). Almost a quarter of the Dutch population cycles every day, traveling an average of 621 miles a year.[23] If you would like to rent a bike, there are plenty of rental places around the city, and some offer guided tours.

Behind-the-Scenes Snapshot: During season 29 we had a long layover in Amsterdam, so Bertram, who was born in the Netherlands, suggested to Phil, Andy (our CBS exec), and me that we take the train from the airport into Amsterdam and rent bikes to ride through Vondelpark. Moments like these are rare for us on *The Amazing Race*, so when they present themselves, we take advantage of them! It was one of the most memorable behind-the-scenes moments that we had while filming the show; riding a bicycle is really the best way to see a city.

Address: Munttoren Tower, Muntplein 12/14, 1012 WR Amsterdam, Netherlands

☐ *Visit the Cheese Market in Alkmaar*
Season 4, Episode 5, Detour

Teams drove to Alkmaar's outdoor market, donned traditional wooden clogs, and used a wooden stretcher to carry cheese from a stockpile to a scale. Once it weighed in at exactly 1,100 pounds of cheese, teams received their next clue.

Alkmaar has the largest cheese market in the Netherlands, which has been in business since 1365. The market is open every Friday from 10:00 a.m. to 1:00 p.m. between April and September. Every seller in the market wears traditional Dutch attire, and the cheese is unloaded, weighed, and sampled according to how it was done more than three hundred years ago.[24] If you would like to purchase cheese, there are many stalls throughout the market where you can buy all kinds of cheese.

Address: Houttil 26, 1811 JM Alkmaar, Netherlands

OTHER HOLLAND MUST-SEES!

- *RIJKSMUSEUM*
- *VONDELPARK*
- *ANNE FRANK'S HOUSE*
- *THE ROYAL PALACE*
- *KEUKENHOF GARDENS IN LISSE*
- *WINDMILLS AT KINDERDIJK*
- *VISIT GIETHOORN, THE VENICE OF THE NETHERLANDS*
- *TAKE A CANAL CRUISE*
- *SEE THE MAGERE BRUG (SKINNY BRIDGE)*

Germany

Berlin

☐ *Visit the Deutsches Technikmuseum*
Season 22, Episode 9, Detour

In the Deutsches Technikmuseum, teams had to build a model train track circuit using all the pieces provided in such a way that the circuit fit on a platform. Once the train made one full lap without falling apart, derailing, or hitting any pieces of scenery, the conductor gave the team their clue.

One of the largest technological museums in Europe, the Deutsches Technikmuseum has hands-on activities, workshops, and exhibits where you can see both new and historical machines of the land, the sea, and the air. Here you can explore the history of ships, fighter planes, steam locomotives, and even computers![25] Make sure you reserve a whole day for this museum—there's so much to see and do!

Address: Deutsches Technikmuseum, Trebbiner Strasse 9, 10963 Berlin, Germany

How to get there: Fly into Berlin Brandenburg Airport, then rent a car or take a taxi.

☐ *Grab a Drink at the Brauhaus Spandau*
Season 6, Episode 5, Detour

At the crowded Brauhaus Spandau bar, both team members had to search the tables for five coasters bearing their team's name and picture. They then had to serve two full beer steins to the patron at the table in exchange for each coaster. Once both team members had collected five of their coasters, they received their next clue.

The Brauhaus Spandau bar opened in 1994 and has been brewing beer in the old Spandau tradition on-site ever since. Prior to being a brewery, the historic building served as an army steam laundry.[26] The large copper brew kettles set in the center of the bar make for a great rustic atmosphere, and even when it's not Oktoberfest, there are always festivities going on inside.[27] Be sure to try the tasty Havelbräu, and depending on the month, try their seasonal beers served with German cuisine.

Address: Neuendorfer Strasse 1, 13585 Berlin, Germany

☐ Walk Through the Brandenburg Gate
Season 6, Episode 5, Pit Stop

At the Saxon State Ministry of Finance in Dresden, teams got into a Ford Fusion and had to answer three questions asked on the MyFord Touch system to reveal their next destination: (1) Who said "Tear down this wall!"? (Ronald Reagan); (2) Who did he say it to? (Mikhail Gorbachev); (3) Where did President Reagan say it? (the Brandenburg Gate in Berlin).

The Brandenburg Gate is one of Germany's most famous landmarks. The gate was built in the eighteenth century and became a symbol of Berlin's and Germany's division during the Cold War; it's now a place of unity and peace.[28] It was at the Brandenburg Gate on June 12, 1987, that Ronald Reagan issued his stern command to his Cold War adversary, admonishing him with the words "Mr. Gorbachev—tear down this wall!"[29]

Address: Pariser Platz, 10117 Berlin, Germany

☐ Stand at the Site of the Berlin Wall
Season 32, Episode 6, Route Marker

Teams arrived by train from Paris and made their way to the wall's East Side Gallery and searched for their clue.

The longest piece left of the Berlin Wall, also known as the East Side Gallery, is also the longest open-air gallery in the world.[30] Consisting of more than one hundred murals painted directly on the wall that caused so much division and oppression, the 4,500-foot-long structure is part of an initiative that preserves works of art; the wall has been restored two times since its creation, once in 2000 and again in 2009.[31]

Behind-the-Scenes Snapshot: In 1990, when I was backpacking through Europe tracing my family history, I visited Berlin, the city where Rudy, my grandfather on my mother's side, was born. He emigrated to New York in 1922 as a seven-year-old, with his family who only spoke German. It wasn't easy, but they were determined to start a new life in a free land. Standing at the Berlin Wall nearly seventy years later, watching people chisel pieces off, taking it down and taking back their freedom, I was struck by the historical moment. The weight of what had happened here and the knowledge of how fortunate we are to have our freedom made an indelible impression on me. These are places we must remember, and we purposely visit them during the race to do so.

Address: Mühlenstrasse 3-100, 10243 Berlin, Germany

Switzerland

Geneva

☐ *Customize Your Own Swiss Army Knife*
Season 28, Episode 4, Detour

At the Victorinox flagship store, teams had to correctly assemble a Victorinox Swiss Army knife from twenty-seven individual pieces to receive their next clue.

Swiss cutler Karl Elsener began supplying a multiuse pocketknife in 1891. This knife was special, as it was equipped with a screwdriver, a blade, a can opener, and a reamer, and it was issued to Swiss soldiers.

Elsener had used a special mechanism to create the first Swiss Army knife, with tools attached to both sides of the handle.[32] At the Victorinox flagship store in Geneva, you can put together your own Swiss Army knife and have it personally engraved.

Address: Rue du Marché 2, 1204 Genève, Switzerland

How to get there: Fly into Geneva Airport (formerly known as Cointrin Airport) and take a taxi or rent a car.

☐ *Sit on One of the Longest Wooden Benches in the World*
Season 28, Episode 4, Detour

At Promenade de la Treille, teams had to determine how many people could sit on the longest wooden bench in the world. Teammates had to measure by sitting next to each other, alternating down the entire length of the bench. If their answer was within the correct range of 190–197, they would receive their next clue. But if they were incorrect, they had to try measuring again.

Behind Geneva's City Hall, high on a hill, is La Treille Park in Old Town. The park's perimeter is lined by (debatably) the longest wooden bench in the world. Built in 1767, the bench is 413 feet long and made of 180 wooden boards. Many countries say they have the longest bench, from Spain's Gaudí-inspired bench to Russia's painted bench that was broken into one hundred pieces and spread all throughout Moscow.[33] No matter where the longest bench lies, the bench at the Promenade de la Treille is one to visit. Make sure to check out the panoramic views and chestnut trees!

Address: Rampe de la Treille 5, Geneva 1204, Switzerland

Grimsel Pass

☐ *Ride the Gelmerbahn Funicular, the Second Steepest Cable Railway in the World*
Season 31, Episode 7, Detour

Teams had to ride the Gelmerbahn funicular. During the ride, they had to memorize eight signs that listed water basins and the amount of water they hold. When their ride ended, teams had to run across a hydroelectric dam and match the eight basin names to their water capacities on a technical map to receive their next clue. Otherwise, they would have to ride the Gelmerbahn again.

With an incline of 106 percent, the Gelmerbahn is the second steepest cable railway in the world. It has become a popular tourist attraction due to its near vertical ascent and descent of the mountainside in open carriages.[34] Once at the top, you will reach the Gelmer Valley, which is six thousand feet above sea level. Up top, you can walk around the turquoise-colored lake, or hike up to the Gelmer Hut for amazing views. The funicular is open from May through October, and is dog friendly as well!

Address: Grimselstrasse 19, 3864 Guttannen, Switzerland

How to get there: Fly into Milan Malpensa Airport or Zurich Airport and take a train or rent a car.

Ticino

☐ *Bungee Jump off the Verzasca Dam*

Season 14, Episode 1, and Season 33,
Episode 5, Roadblock

One team member had to bungee jump off the Verzasca Dam in order to receive their next clue.

Said to be the world's highest stationary bungee jump, the jump off the Verzasca Dam (also known as the Contra Dam) has you falling 721 feet.[35] The bungee jump became especially popular when it was featured in the opening sequence of the 1995 Bond film *GoldenEye*. There are several types of jumps offered: a classic plunge, a backward jump, and if you really want to take it to the next level, you can do a night jump!

Address: Via Valle Verzasca, 6596 Gordola, Switzerland

How to get there: Fly into Milan Malpensa Airport or Zurich Airport and take a train or rent a car.

Italy

Cortina d'Ampezzo

☐ *Take a Ski Lift to the Top of the Dolomite Mountains*

Season 4, Episode 1, Detour

Teams boarded the chairlift at the base of Cinque Torri and rode to the top. Next, teams had to follow a marked path to the clue box.

If you find yourself in the vicinity of Cortina D'Ampezzo, Italy, surrounded by the Dolomite Mountains, then consider visiting Cinque Torri, formed by five towers (which give the group of mountains its name). Cinque Torri has one of the best ski slopes in the area and is part of the Dolomiti Superski area linking the nearby mountain areas.[36] The mountain is open to all levels of skiers and snowboarders from the end of November until the beginning of May. If you're feeling adventurous and can handle a good hike, you can walk up or down the mountain in the summer![37]

Address: Str. Arnaria, 43, 39040 Castelrotto BZ, Italy

How to get there: Fly into Venice Marco Polo Airport and take a bus, taxi, or rent a car.

Venice

☐ ## *Take a Gondola Ride*
Season 4, Episode 2, Detour

Teams had to travel by gondola from Ponte delle Guglie using only a map to guide their gondolier, without asking locals for directions, to Fondazione Querini Stampalia, where they would find their next clue.

Since the eleventh century, gondolas have been weaving through the busy Grand Canal and smaller waterways of Venice. Gondolas often represent romance, history, and tradition, but as time has passed, the number of gondolas sailing through the waterways has decreased, with there only being about four hundred left.[38] Gondoliers are responsible for owning and maintaining their own boats, and the career and craft of sailing is often passed down from father to son.[39] The price to take a gondola ride is fixed, so make sure to discuss where you want to go and how long you want to sail before you start your ride. A good place to find gondolas away from the crowds is in the area of San Polo and Campo San Barnaba.

Ponte delle Guglie Address: Canale di Cannaregio, 30121 Venezia VE, Italy

Fondazione Querini Stampalia Address: Campo Santa Maria Formosa, 5252, 30122 Venezia VE, Italy

How to get there: Fly into Venice Marco Polo Airport and take a bus, taxi, or train; once in Venice, you can take a water taxi.

☐ *Make or Paint a Venetian Mask*
Season 29, Episode 7, Roadblock

At Ca' Zenobio degli Armeni, one team member had to choose an actor from a Venetian masquerade performance, commedia dell'arte, and paint an exact copy of their mask, to the satisfaction of the artist, to receive their next clue.

Mask wearing in Venice can be traced back to the twelfth century, with historians speculating that the initial masks had much to do with the class system in Venice. "The original function of masks in Venice was both practical and aspirational: a person in a mask could be who they wanted to be, and do what they wanted to do. A poor man could be a nobleman for a day. A woman could act like a man, or vice versa."[40] Eventually, it became too much, and the government had to restrict mask wearing to the carnival season. Venetian masks usually fall into two types: carnival masks and commedia dell'arte character masks.[41]

> OTHER VENICE MUST-SEES!
>
> • ST. MARK'S BASILICA
> • ST. MARK'S SQUARE
> • GRAND CANAL
> • RIALTO BRIDGE
> • VISIT MURANO AND WATCH GLASSBLOWING
> • VISIT BURANO FOR LACE
> • GALLERIE DELL'ACCADEMIA

They're traditionally made with papier-mâché, fabric, paint, and jewels, and many classes and workshops are available in Venice where you can make or paint your own carnival mask to take home.

Ca' Zenobio degli Armeni Address: Sestiere Dorsoduro, 2596, 30123 Venezia VE, Italy

Rome

☐ Visit the Pantheon and the Altare della Patria (also known as "the Typewriter")

Season 24, Episode 7, Speed Bump

This Speed Bump required Caroline and Jennifer to head to the Pantheon, pick up an antique Olivetti typewriter, and drop it off at the building it resembled, the Altare della Patria, before they could continue racing.

The Pantheon, one of the best-preserved places in Rome, is thought to have been completed around AD 128.[42] Because it was so long ago, and because there aren't written records, no one knows who designed it. The building has a rotunda with an unsupported dome that to this day is the largest of its kind in the world. At the top of the dome is the oculus, a circular opening about thirty feet across (and the only window in the entire structure).[43] Many famous people are buried in the Pantheon, including artists, poets, and Italy's first two kings. It's free to visit, and the building is conveniently surrounded by small shops and restaurants. Altare della Patria, known to many as "the Typewriter" because of its resemblance to the design of one, is a building with many other names, including Monumento Nazionale a Vittorio Emanuele II (National Monument to Victor Emmanuel II) and Il Vittoriano. The building was built between 1885 and 1925 to honor Victor Emmanuel II; as the first king of unified Italy, he was often referred to as "Father of the Fatherland," and the building's name translates to "Altar of the Fatherland."[44]

Pantheon Address: Piazza della Rotonda, 00186 Rome RM, Italy

Altare della Patria Address: Piazza Venezia, 00186 Rome RM, Italy

How to get there: Fly into Leonardo da Vinci–Fiumicino Airport and take a taxi.

☐ Count the Number of Stairs on the Spanish Steps
Season 24, Episode 7, Roadblock

One team member had to get a postcard from a chestnut vendor and count the stairs of the Spanish Steps, not counting the sidewalk at the bottom. Then they had to add that total to the Roman numerals on the Obelisco Sallustiano in front of the Trinità dei Monti, indicating its year of construction. They had to write down their sum in Roman numerals on the postcard and show it to a pair of impersonators appearing at the top of the steps as Gregory Peck and Audrey Hepburn from *Roman Holiday*. If they had the right answer of MCMXXIV (1,924), they received their next clue.

The Spanish Steps were built in 1725 to connect Piazza di Spagna to the landmark Chiesa (Church) della Trinità dei

> OTHER ROME MUST-SEES!
>
> - COLOSSEUM
> - VATICAN CITY
> - PONTE SANT'ANGELO
> - PIAZZA DEL POPOLO
> - THE ROMAN FORUM
> - TREVI FOUNTAIN
> - PIAZZA NAVONA
> - VILLA BORGHESE
> - THE MOUTH OF TRUTH
>   (BOCCA DELLA VERITA)

Monti. The 135 steps have become a wonderful place to sit and enjoy the views of the city or meet with friends.[45]

Spanish Steps Address: Piazza di Spagna, 00187 Rome RM, Italy

Obelisco Sallustiano Address: Piazza della Trinità dei Monti, 00187 Roma RM, Italy

Austria

Innsbruck

☐ *Visit the Olympic Bobsled Track and Ice Rink*

Season 3, Episode 7, Detour

To receive their next clue teams had the option of riding with professional bobsledders down an Olympic bobsled track at speeds of sixty-five miles per hour or participating in a skating relay with a pair of professional ice skaters on a four-hundred-meter oval at the Olympic ice rink in the Olymphialle (part of the Olympiaworld complex).

The ice chute in Innsbruck was constructed for the 1976 Winter Olympics (which Innsbruck stepped in to host when Denver bowed out), and it's the first of its kind to be a combined track for luge, bobsledding, and skeleton races. Located at the bottom of the Patscherkofel mountain, the track is 4,166 feet long and can give riders a top speed of seventy-four miles per hour. As a visiting rider, you can sit in a five-person bobsled that is piloted by a professional, or you can go headfirst down the run on a skeleton.[46] If you're looking for a unique experience, you can speed down in a giant wok! Although it was constructed for the Winter Olympics, the bobsled run is open in the summer as well.

Built for an earlier Winter Olympics, in 1964, the Olympiahalle was originally a venue for figure skating and ice hockey. Today the venue (also called the Olympic Hall) hosts hockey games, figure skating, curling, short track speed skating, ice stock sport, and more.[47] The venue was also used for the '76 Olympics. Outdoor ice skating is available to the public in the winter months.

Address: Olympiaworld, Olympiastrasse 10, 6020 Innsbruck, Austria

How to get there: Fly into Innsbruck Airport and take a taxi or rent a car.

Vienna

☐ Take a Tour of Schönbrunn Palace
Season 23, Episode 6, Route Marker and Pit Stop

Teams had to search the palace's garden hedge maze for their clue, then make their way on foot to the Pit Stop, the gloriette.

Schönbrunn Palace, built in 1642, is one of Vienna's most important historical landmarks. Set on 460 acres, the palace is a "UNESCO World Cultural Heritage Site" and has a whopping 1,441 rooms, 45 of which you can visit.[48] The palace grounds were also the site of the first-ever zoo, and have the longest orangery in the world at more than six hundred feet. Can you believe that this was built as a summer residence! Mozart even performed here, in 1772, in the Hall of Mirrors. The Schönbrunn Palace park is open to visitors free of charge all year round.

Address: Schönbrunner Schloßstraße 47, 1130 Wien, Austria

How to get there: Fly into Vienna International Airport and take a taxi, train, bus, or rent a car.

☐ *Visit the Site Where Beethoven Wrote the Heiligenstadt Testament*
Season 4, Episode 3, Detour

Teams had to carry a portfolio of sheet music to the house where Ludwig van Beethoven wrote the Heiligenstadt Testament. When they found the right house, a Beethoven impersonator handed them their next clue.

Composer Ludwig van Beethoven was born in Bonn, Germany, but at twenty-one decided to go to Vienna to study music. In a small village outside the city, thirty-two-year-old Beethoven wrote his Heiligenstadt Testament in a time of deep depression; he felt that the only way to come to terms with his depression and deafness was to continue on through his art.[49] Though not originally from Vienna, his life and work are forever connected to the city. You can visit the house where he wrote his testament year-round, as it's now a museum.

Address: Probusgasse 6, 1190 Wien, Austria

☐ *Ride the Wiener Riesenrad (the German Name of the Giant Ferris Wheel in Vienna)*
Season 18, Episode 8, Detour

At the Wiener Riesenrad, teams picked up two large servings of varied forms of traditional Austrian cuisine: Wiener schnitzel, sauerkraut, and Sacher torte. They then boarded one of the Riesenrad's dining cars, where, while a violinist played Viennese music, they would have to finish both servings within one twelve-minute revolution of the Ferris wheel before receiving their next clue. If they did not finish, they would have to start over.

This giant Ferris wheel, built in 1897, is 212 feet tall. Found at the entrance of the Prater Amusement Park, the wheel spins at a speed of 1.7 mph. From the top, you can see amazing views of the city. Individual cabin cars can be booked for exclusive dinners, cocktail receptions, and even weddings.[50] The Giant Ferris Wheel is open all year round.

Address: Riesenradplatz 1, 1020 Wien, Austria

Turkey

Istanbul

☐ *Experience a Traditional Turkish Bath*
Season 21, Episode 6, Detour

Teams had to make their way to the Ayasofya Hürrem Sultan Hamami to partake in a traditional Turkish bath, after which they would receive their next clue from the bath attendants.

The Ayasofya Hürrem Sultan Hamami is a Turkish bath built in 1556 on the site where the Temple of Zeus stood. A Turkish bath, also known as a *hamam*, is a treatment where you sit in a steam room, and then you're rinsed, exfoliated, and massaged.[51] At the height of the Ottoman Empire, every neighborhood of Istanbul had a *hamam* with hot and cold baths, fountains, and domed marble rooms. For the past one thousand years, the *hamam* tradition has been important for cleanliness and health, but also for entertainment and social gatherings.[52]

Address: Cankurtaran, Ayasofya Meydanı No:2, 34122 Fatih/Istanbul, Turkey

How to get there: Fly into Istanbul Airport and take a taxi or rent a car.

> *OTHER ISTANBUL MUST-SEES!*
>
> - *AYA SOFYA*
> - *YENI MOSQUE (THE NEW MOSQUE)*
> - *BASILICA CISTERN*
> - *RUMELI HISARI*
> - *TOPKAPI PALACE*
> - *YEDIKULE FORTRESS*
> - *GALATA TOWER*
> - *USKUDAR FERRY*
> - *KIZ KULESI (MAIDEN'S TOWER)*
> - *MISIR CARSISI (SPICE BAZAAR)*

☐ Visit the Kapalıçarşi (Grand Bazaar)
Season 21, Episode 6, Roadblock

At the Kapalıçarşi, one team member had to sell and serve forty glasses of sherbet (Turkish soda) poured from a long-spouted brass teapot called an *ibrik*. Once they earned ₺40 (approx. US $20), they received their next clue.

The bazaar opened in 1461 and is one of the oldest and largest covered markets in the world. It resembles a giant labyrinth, containing twenty-one gates and over fifty-six passageways. There are 4,400 shops, 25,000 full-time staff, 61 covered streets, and even mosques and fountains![53] Its high ceiling is covered with a dome that consists of hundreds of windows (and is a stunning sight to see).

Address: Beyazıt, Kalpakçılar Cd. No:22, 34126 Fatih/Istanbul, Turkey

Season 1. In Anchorage, Alaska,
Margarita rides a dogsled and takes the lead.

Image Credit: ViacomCBS

Season 28. Korey takes a shot at Fowling in Detroit, Michigan.

Image Credit: ViacomCBS

Season 1. First-time contestants take off on a race around the world, starting from the Bethesda Fountain in New York City!

< Image Credit: ViacomCBS

Season 23. In Juneau, Alaska, teams fly in bush planes over Mendenhall Glacier.

Image Credit: Chad Baron >

Season 24. For this Speed Bump, one team had to bring an antique typewriter to the building it resembles— the Altare della Patria, which locals call "the Typewriter."

Image Credit: ViacomCBS

Season 26. Hayley and Blair share a HotTug ride in the Amsterdam canals.

Image Credit: ViacomCBS

Season 6. Crossing the Vatnajökull Glacier in Iceland.

Image Credit: ViacomCBS

Season 25. In London, England, teams had to make their way
to Tower Bridge to receive their next clue.

Image Credit: ViacomCBS

Season 27. Co-creators and executive producers
Bertram van Munster and Elise Doganieri stand at the
Arc de Triomphe Pit Stop in Paris, France.

Image Credit: Elise Doganieri

Season 6. The Brandenburg Gate in Berlin was the Pit Stop for season 6.

Season 28. In this Chamonix, France, Roadblock, one contestant had to perform a tandem paraglide from seven thousand feet.

Season 6. In Oslo, Norway, one team member had to climb to the top of the Holmenkollen ski jump and then ride a zip line to the bottom to receive their next clue.

Image Credit: Elise Doganieri

Seasons 14 & 33. Jumping 721 feet off the Verzasca Dam in Ticino, Switzerland, takes nerves of steel!

Image Credit: ViacomCBS >

Season 23. At Schönbrunn Palace in Vienna, Austria, teams had to search the giant hedge maze for their next clue.

Image Credit: ViacomCBS

Season 24. At the Spanish Steps in Rome, Italy, teams had to count the steps as part of their next task.

Image Credit: ViacomCBS >

Season 4. In Venice, Italy, teams traveled by gondola, directing their gondolier to their next location using only a map.

< Image Credit: ViacomCBS

Season 2. Teams hang glide from the top of Pedra Bonita down to São Conrado Pepino Beach in Rio de Janeiro, Brazil.

Image Credit: ViacomCBS

Season 2. Chris and Alex read a map at the base of Christ the Redeemer in Rio de Janeiro, Brazil.

< Image Credit: ViacomCBS

AFRICA

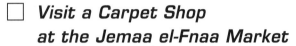

Morocco

Marrakech

☐ *Visit a Carpet Shop at the Jemaa el-Fnaa Market*
Season 3, Episode 6, Fast Forward

This Fast Forward required one team to look through piles of carpets in a Marrakech carpet shop to find the one with the Fast Forward design sewn into it.

The Jemaa el-Fnaa is Marrakech's main square and marketplace in the old city, and is a place where locals and tourists gather. During the day, the square is full of vendors selling orange juice, spices, and medicines from their stalls. At night, the main square transforms and the stalls disappear to make room for acrobats, snake charmers, and henna tattoo artists.[1] Food stands open and visitors can have dinner surrounded by musicians playing traditional Moroccan music. The medina market streets are where you can buy just about anything, from the smallest of souvenirs to furniture, clothing, and rugs. Each rug is handmade by local men and women all over Morocco, and each one tells a different story.[2] Bargaining is all part of the game when you want to purchase anything, so be ready to make a deal!

Behind-the-Scenes Snapshot: I remember my first time in Marrakech—I was scouting season 2 and wanted to purchase a small rug to bring home. I didn't quite understand the process of negotiation. In Marrakech, haggling is the means by which you purchase goods in the medina, and a highly charged negotiation is *expected* (so don't be alarmed when the haggling begins). This experience of course instantly inspired some creative thinking for this *Amazing Race* challenge.

Address: Rue El Ksour, 38, Marrakech 40000, Morocco

How to get there: Fly into Marrakech Menara Airport and take a taxi.

☐ *Stay in a Riad*
Season 3, Episode 6, Pit Stop

A traditional Moroccan house, also known as a *riad*, is a house built with an inner courtyard or garden. All the rooms in the house have windows that face into the courtyard to further the Islamic idea of inward reflection and privacy.[3] Inadvertently, the design helps to keep the air cool and comfortable, which can be very helpful during hot summers. *Riads* are popular structures all over Morocco, but in the Old Medina of Marrakech, you will find some of the most authentic ones. The most sought-after *riads* are usually located within a ten-minute walk of Jemaa el-Fnaa.[4]

Address: Riad Catalina, 21 Derb Abdellah Ben Hssaine Bab Laksour, Marrakech 40000 Morocco

☐ *Ride Quad Bikes Through the Desert*
Season 3, Episode 6, Detour

Teams chose one quad (sand) bike and rode to a Route Marker to find a clue etched in Arabic on a stone. Once there, they made a rubbing of the clue on a piece of paper and had to translate it to reveal their next location.

Several adventure companies offer quad bike tours. Professional guides are available for half-day, full-day, or even multi-day tours. Explore the Agafay desert, located south of Marrakech, for views of the Atlas Mountains, or the Jbilets desert, located along the famous Palmeraie of Marrakech, north of the city.[5]

☐ Have a Moroccan Mint Tea at the Palais Gharnata
Season 25, Episode 5, Detour

Teams had to properly serve Moroccan mint tea. After picking up a traditional tea set that included a sugar box, mint tea, green tea, and a samovar, they then made their way to the Palais Gharnata, where they got into costume and observed how to properly serve the tea. While one team member held the serving tray steady with one hand, the other had to ceremonially pour the tea into two cups at once, making sure to lift the kettles up to a particular height, to receive their next clue.

The Gharnata Palace was built in the sixteenth century and is situated between the Bahia Palace, the prefecture of the medina (non-European quarter), and the Dar Si Said Museum. The grounds, walls, pillars, and doors are all specially crafted with wood, painted and carved in seven colors. This is all done in compliance with Arabic geometry.[6] The palace serves Moroccan-style food to dine on, but do make sure to grab a cup of mint tea at the beginning or end of your meal. Morocco's famous mint tea, steeped with spearmint, is symbolic of Moroccan hospitality and culture. Locals enjoy this sweet drink throughout the day, and when a guest comes to visit they can ex-

OTHER MARRAKECH MUST-SEES!

- KOUTOUBIA MOSQUE
- SAADIAN TOMBS
- BADI PALACE
- TANNERIES
- ALMORAVID KOUBBA
- BEN YOUSSEF MADRASA
- MANARA GARDENS

pect to be offered tea as a welcoming gesture. Be sure to lift the teapot high above the cup while pouring; Moroccans do this as a way to aerate the tea.[7]

Address: Palais Gharnata, 5,6 Derb El Arsa Riad Zitoun Jdid, Marrakech 40040, Morocco

Egypt

Giza

☐ *See the Sphinx*
Season 5, Episode 5, Pit Stop

The Great Sphinx of Giza is one of the largest sculptures in the world, coming in at 240 feet long and 66 feet high. The limestone sculpture features a lion's body and the head of King Khafre (estimated to have been built c. 2500 BC). The statue was carved from a single piece of limestone, and pigment residue suggests that the entire Sphinx was painted.[8] Some think it may have taken over three years and one hundred people to create the sculpture, using stone hammers and copper chisels.[9]

Address: Al Giza Desert, Giza Governorate, Egypt

How to get there: Fly into Cairo International Airport and take a taxi.

☐ *Visit the Great Pyramid*
Season 5, Episode 5, Roadblock

At the Great Pyramid, one team member had to descend into the Osiris Shaft, through a claustrophobic and deep chamber, to retrieve a satchel with puzzle pieces and bring it to the Egyptologist back at the surface to receive their next clue.

The Great Pyramid of Giza, built on the West Bank of the Nile River, is one of the oldest and largest pyramids in history, dating back to 2560 BC.[10] The profound structure, built by the pharaoh Khufu, stands at 481 feet tall and consists of 2.3 million blocks of limestone and granite, all of which were individually cut, moved, and assembled.[11] There are two tunnel systems in the Great Pyramid, a lower one (which is common among other pyramids of the time) and an upper one (which was very carefully hidden and something that was not common). Tourists can enter all three of the great pyramids, but the Great Pyramid of Khufu is a bit claustrophobic, since visitors must scramble a long way through tight passages. Many people who visit the Giza Plateau choose to go on a camel ride around the Pyramids. If you choose to ride just before sunset, you will have a magnificent view of the Pyramids and be able to hear the Call to Prayer rising from hundreds of mosques at the same time.[12]

Behind-the-Scenes Snapshot: Egypt is a place I've dreamed of visiting since I was a child. When I was ten, my grandparents bought me a subscription to *National Geographic* magazine. I remember anticipating its arrival in the mail every month. In March 1977, an edition arrived with a photo of Tutankhamun's gold mask on the cover, and I was so intrigued. I read the magazine cover to cover and knew I would visit Egypt one day. Seeing the pyramids for the first time, I was awestruck; I couldn't believe I was standing in the place where pharaohs once walked. To be granted access to film on the Giza Plateau and to have our Pit Stop right at the base of the Sphinx was truly a dream come true.

Address: Al Haram, Nazlet El-Semman, Al Giza Desert, Giza Governorate, Egypt

Luxor

☐ Take a Felucca on the Nile

Season 5, Episode 6, Detour

Teams had to travel to Banana Island and load ten sheep onto a traditional boat known as a felucca, then sail across to the west bank of the Nile River, and deliver the sheep to a shepherd in exchange for their next clue.

Feluccas are simple, traditional Egyptian sailboats that have traveled the Nile River since ancient times. Many feluccas have been adapted to carry between eight to twelve people comfortably. Being wind-powered craft with no motor, feluccas are dependent on the breeze to propel them forward; this quiet journey is a wonderful way to watch the sunset on an evening tour.[13]

Address: Banana Island, Al Aqaletah, Al Qarna, Luxor Governorate, Egypt

How to get there: Fly into Luxor International Airport and take a taxi.

Tanzania

Zanzibar

☐ **Take a Ferry**
from Dar es Salaam to Zanzibar
Season 29, Episode 3, Route Marker

At the Askari Monument in Dar es Salaam, teams had to search through the classifieds in a newspaper for one with a picture of a boat telling them to travel by ferry to Zanzibar.

To get to Zanzibar from Dar es Salaam by ferry, you will want to make sure to buy your ferry ticket in advance (as it's very busy, especially during travel season).[14] The Dar ferry station is located on the waterfront in downtown and takes two to three hours to arrive in Zanzibar. At the ferry dock in Zanzibar, you will have to pass through immigration and then proceed out of the official port, so be sure to bring your passport!

Address: Azam Marine & Kilimanjaro Fast Ferries, Opposite St. Joseph Cathedral, Sokoine Drive, Dar es Salaam, Tanzania

How to get there: Fly into Julius Nyerere International Airport and take a taxi to the ferry.

☐ Visit Stone Town and Find the Royal Doors

Season 29, Episode 4, Detour

Teams had to travel through the streets of Stone Town to locate three royal doors, each of which would be distinguished by a carving on top of either a lion, a serpent, or a falcon, and knock on each door to receive another wooden carving. After collecting all three carvings, teams then had to deliver them to a marked shop on Gizenga Street to receive their next clue.

A famous feature of Zanzibar architecture is the carved wooden door; these doors illustrate the blending of cultures that occurred in the area's history. The heavy doors are usually associated with Swahili culture, which also often includes Middle Eastern, European, Arab, and Asian cultures. You can see Arab influence in the shape of some of the older doors. The newer doors often reflect Indian culture. Here, the door is usually the first item built when constructing a house, "a tradition that originates from the Persian Gulf region and by the 15th century had reached Zanzibar."[15] The doors often reflected the wealth of the families living behind them. The remaining doors (approximately 560) primarily date from the eighteenth and nineteenth centuries and are carefully monitored and maintained by the Stone Town Conservation and Development Authority.[16]

How to get there: Fly into Julius Nyerere International Airport and take a taxi to the ferry terminal, then take the ferry to Zanzibar.

☐ Find Freddie Mercury's Childhood Home

Season 29, Episode 4, Route Marker

At the start of the leg, teams were instructed to find the house of "Farrokh Bulsara," who they would figure out was known to the rest of the world as Freddie Mercury, and travel to his childhood home in Stone Town for their next clue.

Freddie Mercury (Farrokh Bulsara) was born in Stone Town in 1946. The legendary front man of Queen lived in this home with his sister and their parents, who had emigrated from India.[17] The first-ever museum dedicated to Freddie is located in the home he grew up in (until his parents moved to England in 1963). Here, you can see photos and walk the hallways and rooms that Freddie once inhabited.[18]

Address: Kenyatta Road, Zanzibar City, Tanzania

☐ *Visit the Darajani Market*
Season 29, Episode 3, Roadblock

At the Darajani Market, one team member received a shopping list of eighteen local food items, with some of the items written in Swahili. Using their own money (either United States dollars or Tanzanian shillings), to receive the next clue they had to purchase all the items and give the ingredients to a local waiting for their groceries outside the market.

This main market in Zanzibar is constantly buzzing with many things to buy—from meat and fresh fish to toys and mobile phones—there's something for everyone within these covered stalls.[19] It's best to go earlier in the day if you're looking to buy food and groceries, as everything is very fresh in the morning (it's busiest in the morning, but definitely worth it). The market extends to the outside, with vendors selling items like bread, clothing, or even household goods. Make sure to visit the area known as Kanga Street, where shops sell colorful local prints and fabrics of all kinds.[20]

Address: Market Street, Zanzibar, Tanzania

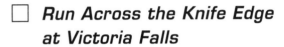

Zambia

Victoria Falls

☐ *Run Across the Knife Edge at Victoria Falls*

Season 1, Episode 1, Route Marker

The Knife Edge Bridge in the midst of Victoria Falls was the first-ever location visited in the entire series of *The Amazing Race*.

The largest waterfall in Zambia, Victoria Falls is also one of the seven natural wonders of the world.[21] The Zambezi River forms the border between Zimbabwe and Zambia, and four hundred feet above is the Knife Edge that links the two countries. Be prepared to get soaked if you plan to walk the length of the bridge, as the rain and spray are the most exciting part!

Address: Livingstone, Zambia

How to get there: Fly into Harry Mwanga Nkumbula International Airport and take a taxi or rent a car.

☐ *Fly in a Microlight Plane over Victoria Falls*

Season 27, Episode 4, Roadblock

One member from each team had to choose a microlight plane and fly above Victoria Falls to spot the Route Marker below the mist on the Knife

Edge Bridge. Once they landed, they reunited with their partner and traveled to the bridge, where they would find their next clue.

While you may want to experience the waterfall up close and walk the bridge, there's also the option to see it from above! You can take in the breathtaking views as you circle over the waterfall and the spectacular gorge that the Zambezi River has carved into the surrounding landscape over thousands of years (all in a microlight plane!).[22] Microlights are completely open-air, giving you the feeling of actually flying like a bird. They can also fly lower than helicopters can, giving you a real close-up on the falls. There are companies in the area that specialize in these planes—do your research and find the company that feels the best to you. Your hotel should also have recommendations!

Behind-the-Scenes Snapshot: We had been to Victoria Falls during season 1 and knew we would go back, but this time we wanted to see it from a bird's-eye view. During the scout, we decided to check out the microlight flight over Victoria Falls, and I volunteered to take the test flight. I had only seen photos of microlight aircraft, so when I saw it in person and it looked like a beach chair connected to three wheels and a lawn mower engine, I was nervous, to say the least! I'm always up for an adventure, but I have to say it took me a few minutes to gather the courage to fly. Microlights are completely open to the air, so you fly like a bird, feeling every gust of wind and, in this case, sprays of water from the falls. I knew once I took off that this was a necessary addition to the race.

☐ Go on a Game Drive at Mosi-Oa-Tunya National Park
Season 1, Episode 2, Detour

Teams had to go to Mosi-oa-Tunya National Park and use an instant camera to photograph three hard-to-find animals from a provided list of five (giraffe, impala, water buffalo, zebra, rhino).

Mosi-oa-Tunya National Park is Zambia's smallest national park. Established in 1972 out of the desire to have all species native to Zambia in one place, the national park extends from the Batoka Gorge along the Zambezi River, above Victoria Falls.[23] This park is unique, as it's the only place in Zambia that you can see white rhinos; they're closely looked over by scouts to protect them from poachers. In addition to rhinos, you may see elephants, giraffes, buffalos, waterbucks, impalas, wildebeests, zebras, bushbucks, warthogs, monkeys, baboons, hippos, and crocodiles![24]

Behind-the-Scenes Snapshot: My first trip to Africa was in 1997 when I was working with Bertram on a show called *Wild Things*. We had plans to go to Nairobi National Park on a game drive on the first morning; I was almost laughed out of the safari vehicle when I showed up in bright white (I had no idea there were specific colors you shouldn't wear). I learned that you never want to wear bright colors, as they attract attention; you shouldn't wear camouflage unless you're in the military; and dark colors attract tsetse flies. The best color to wear is khaki, as it blends into the environment. This game drive was one of the most enthralling experiences of my life—I knew when we were brainstorming ideas for *The Amazing Race* that this would be a unique experience for the teams!

Address: Livingstone, Kazungula District, Southern Province

How to get there: Fly into Livingstone Airport then transfer to Kenneth Kaunda International Airport, and from there you can take a taxi, hire a car and driver, or rent a car.

Zimbabwe Border

☐ Jump by Rope Swing into the Batoka Gorge

Season 27, Episode 5, Roadblock
(inspired by the Batoka Gorge swing set up
for *The Amazing Race* in Season 1)

This leg's Roadblock was a switchback to the very first Detour from season 1. One team member had to strap on a harness, free-fall two hundred feet into the Batoka Gorge, and swing above the Zambezi River. Once they returned to the top, they got their next clue. (The jump for *Amazing Race* 27 had taken place on the Zimbabwe side of the gorge.)

The Batoka Gorge is just a few miles outside Livingstone and just below the cascade of Victoria Falls. The deep, narrow gorge has a depth of up to one thousand feet in certain areas and straddles the border between Zambia and Zimbabwe; guides are often talking and yelling about the "Zim Side" or the "Zam Side."[25] Leap off the platform into the wide-open air as you plunge into the mouth of the Batoka Gorge! You'll free-fall about 229 feet and then begin a pendulum swing that will take your breath away!

How to get there: Fly into Livingstone Airport and take a taxi or rent a car.

Maun (Okavango Delta)

☐ *Go on a Horseback Safari*

Season 22, Episode 7, Detour

Teams had to go on a horseback safari at the Royal Tree Lodge and spot ten wooden animal cutouts: zebra, African buffalo, kudu, giraffe, meerkat, boomslang snake, leopard, warthog, ostrich, and a hippopotamus with a heron. They then traveled to a nearby campsite and arranged a set of tiles featuring the silhouettes of the animals in the order they appeared. There were tiles for animals they did not see, and none of the tiles represented the hippopotamus, but there was one for the heron. Once the team arranged the tiles in the right order, they received their next clue; if they couldn't, they had to go back to the safari before being allowed another attempt to arrange the tiles.

Botswana is considered one of the best places on Earth to partake in a horse-riding safari; the country has a huge array of wildlife, and scenery that is unmatched. On horseback, you're able to see a variety of landscapes, from harsh, dry desert to delta wetlands.[26] There are three main areas for horseback safari in Botswana: the Okavango Delta, the Makgadikgadi Salt Pans, and the Mashatu Reserve along the Limpopo River. In the Okavango Delta flood months, these horseback safaris offer the unique experience of crossing the flooded plains.[27]

Address: Royal Tree Lodge, Royal Tree Lodge Boulevard, Maun, Ngamiland East, Botswana

How to get there: Fly into Maun Airport and take a taxi.

☐ Explore the Okavango Delta in a Makoro

Season 22, Episode 7, Roadblock

On the banks of the Thamalakane River, one team member had to transport two goats downriver to a delivery point using a makoro, a traditional dugout canoe. The team member performing the Roadblock had to propel the canoe forward by standing and using a long wooden pole to push off the bottom of the riverbed, while their partner would look after the goats. Once the goats were delivered, they would receive their next clue.

The makoro is a popular mode of transportation in the Okavango Delta. Originally the only form of transport for fishing or moving people, it was crafted from tree trunks; changing with the times, the modern makoro is now constructed from molded fiberglass.[28] Using a long pole called a *ngashi* to punt the makoro forward is a wonderful way to experience the sounds and sights of wildlife without scaring off animals with a motorized vehicle.[29] The ride is a photographer's dream, and the guides are highly knowledgeable about the area and the wildlife you will encounter as you travel the river. Choose one of the many available guides, or ask your hotel for a recommendation.

South Africa

Cape Town

☐ *Visit the Victoria & Alfred Waterfront*
Season 2, Episode 3, Route Marker

Teams arrived in Cape Town and traveled to the Victoria & Alfred Waterfront. Here they took the ferry to Robben Island.

The oldest working harbor in the southern hemisphere, the Victoria & Alfred Waterfront (named after Queen Victoria and her son Prince Alfred) sees millions of visitors every year.[30] With Table Mountain as its backdrop, you can dine at the many cafés and restaurants, shop in the 450 retail stores, and enjoy exciting activities such as the Cape Ferris wheel or a boat charter.

Address: V & A Waterfront, 19 Dock Road, Cape Town 8001, South Africa

How to get there: Fly into Cape Town International Airport and take a taxi, bus, or rent a car.

☐ *Go to Robben Island and Visit Nelson Mandela's Prison Cell*
Season 2, Episode 3, Route Marker

Once in Cape Town, to retrieve the next clue teams took a ferry to Robben Island and had to find Nelson Mandela's prison cell, where he was incarcerated for eighteen years in Section B, Cell 5.

Robben Island is located five miles off the shore of Cape Town and is considered "a testament to courage and fortitude in the face of brutality."[31] Between the seventeenth and twentieth centuries, Robben Island was a place for banishment and isolation, but today it's a World Heritage Site and Museum (which opened just three years after the fall of Apartheid). A visit to Robben Island is a reminder of the price that so many people paid for freedom. You can take a tour and visit Mandela's cell, a seven-by-nine-foot room where he was held prisoner for eighteen years. Many guides are former prisoners, and they speak openly about their lives inside this historical prison.[32]

Behind-the-Scenes Snapshot: It has always been part of the fabric that makes up the beautiful tapestry of *The Amazing Race* to take the viewer and our contestants to historically important locations that help us remember and reflect on what occurred there. Whether you learn about something in school, by reading a book, or by watching the show, Bertram and I feel it's important never to forget our history and the places and people who came before us to shape our world. Nelson Mandela is one of those people, and standing in his prison cell was one of those important moments.

Address: The Nelson Mandela Gateway to Robben Island, Victoria & Albert Waterfront, Cape Town 8001, South Africa

How to get there: Take a ferry from the Nelson Mandela Gateway at the Victoria & Albert Waterfront.

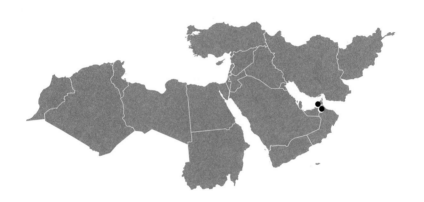

MIDDLE EAST

United Arab Emirates

Dubai

☐ ***Virtually Jump off the Tallest Skyscraper in the World***

Season 31, Episode 5, Detour

Teams made their way to the Burj Khalifa and chose a jumpmaster, who would take them to the 125th floor. There, teams would discover that they had to don a virtual reality headset and virtually parachute to the base of the building. After the jump, to receive their next clue both team members had to correctly answer a test based on what they'd seen on the way down.

The Burj Khalifa skyscraper in Dubai is the world's tallest building. Completed in 2009, its height remained a secret until construction was completed. The building has 162 floors and stands at 2,722 feet, more than half a mile.[1] The virtual reality jump is located on the 125th floor and is designed to test your fear of jumping off the world's tallest building! The VR booths provide a multisensory experience, with physical 4D cues, 360 spatial sound, and simulated wind to deepen the immersion.[2]

Address: Burj Khalifa 1, Mohammed Bin Rashid Boulevard, Downtown Dubai, United Arab Emirates

How to get there: Fly into Dubai International Airport and take a taxi or rent a car.

☐ *Tandem Skydive over the Desert*
Season 5, Episode 8, Detour

Teams had to tandem skydive with an instructor from ten thousand feet to a landing site in the Margham Dunes. When they landed, they would get their next clue.

A tandem skydive is the quickest and most exciting way to experience the thrill of free fall. From ten thousand feet, you will drop at 120 mph; the free fall will last about sixty seconds, and then once the parachute is deployed, you will have a relaxing descent that lasts anywhere between four to five minutes.[3] Before doing a tandem skydive over Dubai's sand dunes, make sure you do your research to figure out which company best fits your needs.

The Margham Dunes are located about twenty-two miles from the city center of Dubai.

☐ *Enjoy a Four-by-Four Adventure in the Golden Dunes of the Margham Desert*
Season 5, Episode 8, Detour

Teams had to travel directly to the Margham Dunes, within the Dubai Desert Conservation Reserve, where they had to drive a marked four-by-four over a six-mile course through the desert, ending at the skydiving landing site.

The Dubai Desert Conservation Reserve is the UAE's first national park. The reserve goes on for sixty miles across the sand and was established to protect the desert ecosystem when Dubai was starting to be developed into the city that stands today.[4] Four different tour operators have been granted permission to operate in the park, offering dune driving excursions, camel riding, and falconry displays, as well as Bedouin-style dining and traditional entertainment. Riding a four-by-four here can best be described as a roller-coaster ride on the sand![5]

If this is something you're interested in doing, reach out to one of the four operators to make your way into the park.

☐ *Visit the Dubai Frame*
Season 31, Episode 5, Detour

Teams traveled to the Dubai Frame and made their way to the top of the tower to find their next clue.

The Dubai Frame is one of the city's architectural marvels. The landmark is designed and positioned to allow one to see modern Dubai framed in the landmark when looking through it from one side, and to see the older parts of the city when looking through it from the other side. Shaped like a photo frame, the side towers each measure 492 feet in height, and the bridge connecting the two measures 305 feet across.[6] One of the best features of the bridge is that the frosted glass below your feet turns clear, allowing you to see the city under you. The frame is covered in gold, a nod to Dubai being the center of gold trading.[7]

Address: Zabeel Park Jogging Track—Za'abeelAl Kifaf, Dubai, United Arab Emirates

☐ *Hit the Slopes at Ski Dubai*
Season 15, Episode 5, Detour

The Detour was a choice between "Build a Snowman" or "Find a Snowman." In "Build a Snowman," the team had to take snow from Ski Dubai and carry it outside, where the temperature was approximately 120°F. They then had to build a snowman, complete with two coal eyes, a carrot nose, and a top hat, before the snow melted. If the snowman was to the attendant's satisfaction, they would hand the team their next clue. In "Find a Snowman," teams had to ride a ski lift to the top of the artificial mountain, sled down to the bottom, and search for a toy snowman buried in the snow. When the team found one, they had to give it to a person in a polar bear suit in exchange for their next clue.

You can find one of the world's largest indoor ski slopes in the middle of the desert at Ski Dubai. Test your snowboarding or skiing skills down one of the five different trails available, each a different level of difficulty.[8]

Address: Sheikh Zayed Road—Al Barsha 1, Dubai, United Arab Emirates

☐ *Race a Car at the Dubai Autodrome*
Season 15, Episode 5, Fast Forward

Teams traveled to the Dubai Autodrome, where one team member had to drive a Formula Three open-wheel race car a single lap around the track in forty-five seconds or less. The first team to do so would win the Fast Forward award and would be driven to the Pit Stop in a Maserati.

At Dubai Autodrome, you can experience an extreme adrenaline rush and make your race-car-driving dreams come true! There's something for every level of driver, and even non-drivers who still want to experience the thrill. Choose between a Ferrari GT, a McLaren MP4-12C, and more. Alternatively, get into the passenger seat while one of their race instructors takes you around the track at high speed![9]

Address: Sheikh Mohammed Bin Zayed Road, Motor City, Dubai, United Arab Emirates

☐ *Visit the Gold Souk and Shop for Gold*
Season 15, Episode 6, Detour

Teams had to find Deepu Jewellers in the Gold Souk of Dubai's Deira area, where they would use a precision scale to weigh out $500,000 worth of gold to the nearest ounce to receive their next clue. The price of gold per ounce was displayed on a television monitor but would change by the minute.

Dubai's Gold Souk is the largest gold market in the world, and today is one of the world's busiest, with over three hundred shops to choose from. The Gold Souk started when Indian and Iranian traders began setting up stalls in the area, with most stalls selling gold, platinum, or diamonds.[10] Make sure to negotiate, as visitors shopping for gold can get incredible deals, but even non-shoppers will be impressed by the sheer spectacle of the Gold Souk. Feel free to wander on your own, or book a tour to learn more about the space as you walk through.

Address: Sikkat Al-Khali Street, Deira, Dubai, United Arab Emirates

☐ *Visit Dubai Garden Glow*
Season 31, Episode 5, Detour

Teams had to make their way to Dubai Garden Glow and don Tyrannosaurus rex costumes. They then had to search Dinosaur Park for a white, a red, a purple, a blue, and a green glowing dinosaur egg and place the eggs in a nest to receive their next clue.

Dubai Garden Glow is the largest glow park in the world. There are many sections to the park, including the Glow Park, the Dinosaur Park, the Ice Park, and the Art Park; make sure to check out all of them, as they each offer something extraordinarily different! You can see all the installations during the day, but at night is when the park really comes to life, with hundreds of sculptures and art installations glowing in bright colors. Built with the environment in mind, the park uses millions of energy-saving LED lights and yards of recycled fabric to create these magical pieces.[11] You can also walk through light tunnels and experience the park's interactive pieces. This is a wonderful place to bring the whole family.

Behind-the-Scenes Snapshot: When we filmed this Detour, we made an arrangement to reserve our own section of the park, while leaving the rest of the park open to guests. Unfortunately, the owner didn't inform his employees, and they opened our filming section to visitors. For the challenge, we'd created giant glowing dinosaur eggs that we hid all around the park, and just before the teams arrived, we noticed some were missing! Kids had picked them up and were running all around the park with them; they thought they were part of the park, so we had to scramble to find all the eggs and put them back in place before the teams arrived! We had our own mini Amazing Race behind the scenes just before teams showed up.

Address: Zabeel Park, Gate Nos. 6 & 7 Area B, Dubai, United Arab Emirates

☐ *Ride on the World's Longest Urban Zip Line*
Season 31, Episode 5, Pit Stop

Teams had to make their way to the top of the Amwaj Tower and ride the world's longest urban zip line to the Pit Stop at the Dubai Marina.

Take off from the top of Amwaj Tower and soar 557 feet above the Dubai skyline for more than half a mile. Flying over land and water, this zip line has multiple lines, so you can ride in tandem with your friends and family![12]

Address to check in: Dubai Marina Mall (Level P), Sheikh Zayed Road, Dubai Marina, Dubai, United Arab Emirates

☐ Take the Plunge on the Leap of Faith Waterslide

Season 15, Episode 6, Route Marker

After the Detour, teams made their way to the Atlantis, the Palm resort on the Palm Jumeirah peninsula. There, both team members had to slide down the resort's Leap of Faith waterslide, which dropped them six stories down a nearly ninety-degree incline and through a tunnel beneath the aquarium's shark lagoon. At the bottom, teams found their next clue, which instructed the pair to search the grounds of Dolphin Bay Beach for the Pit Stop.

On the property of Atlantis, the Palm is the Atlantis Aquaventure, home to one of the scariest waterslides in the world. The resort has thirty waterslides, Dubai's longest lazy river, and a private beach! The Leap of Faith has a sixty-foot near-vertical drop through shark-filled waters (this is the same height as a nine-story building!).[13]

Address: Crescent Road, Atlantis the Palm, Dubai, United Arab Emirates

☐ Take the Plunge on the Poseidon's Revenge Waterslide

Season 28, Episode 8, Route Marker

After the Roadblock, teams had to slide down the Poseidon's Revenge waterslide at the Atlantis Aquaventure water park (which featured a recall from season 15) to receive their next clue.

On the same grounds of the Leap of Faith is Poseidon's Revenge, a waterslide with the title of "most frightening in the Middle East"; it's guaranteed to have your heart pounding and adrenaline at an all-time high. As you step into the launching capsule, the clear walls will be closed on you as you're standing on a trapdoor. Once that door below your feet opens, you will be plummeted more than 100 feet, falling through the loops of the 390-foot waterslide.[14] Expect to free-fall at almost 40 mph, and prepare to even be propelled upside down!

Address: Crescent Road, Atlantis, the Palm, Dubai, United Arab Emirates

Al Ain

☐ *See 147,000 Date Palms at Al Ain Oasis*
Season 23, Episode 8, Detour

At Al Ain Oasis, teams had to search for their next clue, which was located at the top of one of several date palm trees. When they located the right tree, they had to ask for help from the local tree climbers to retrieve the clue.

The luscious Al Ain Oasis, located in the center of Al Ain (Abu Dhabi's Garden City), covers three thousand acres and has an ancient irrigation system that taps faraway underground and mountain aquifers that supply necessary water to the 150,000 date palms.[15] Since 2011, Al Ain Oasis has been a UNESCO World Heritage Site, but only with recent developments is it now open to the public. Visit Al Ain Oasis to see what agriculture in this region has looked like for millennia as you walk under the shade of the palm trees.[16]

Address: Central District, near the Al Ain Palace Museum, Abu Dhabi, United Arab Emirates

How to get there: From Dubai you can take a taxi or rent a car.

☐ *Ride Down the World's Largest Man-Made River Rapids*

Season 23, Episode 8, Roadblock

At Wadi Adventure, team members had to ride down the largest man-made river rapids in the world and collect three flags each, colored red, green, and black, to receive their next clue.

The family-friendly Wadi Adventure park is home to the Middle East's first man-made white-water rafting river. The river extends more than 3,600 feet in length, and is the perfect place to go kayaking or rafting. The grounds also feature a ropes course, a 3,900-foot zip line, a giant swing, a surfing wall, pools, and wakeboarding facilities.[17]

Address: Mbazzarah Al Khadra, Abu Dhabi, United Arab Emirates

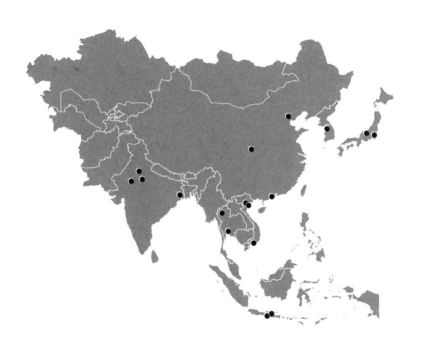

ASIA

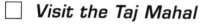

India

Agra

☐ *Visit the Taj Mahal*
Season 1, Episode 8, Route Marker

At the world-famous Taj Mahal, teams had to search the expansive grounds for their next clue, which instructed them to travel to Jaipur's Hawa Mahal.

The Taj Mahal, the most recognized structure in India, was erected in 1632 by the Mughal emperor Shah Jahan to house the remains of his deceased wife. The large mausoleum was built over the span of twenty years, and is a true vision of Mughal architecture, which combines Indian, Persian, and Islamic influences.[1] The Taj Mahal took more than twenty thousand workers and one thousand elephants to build, and is a representation of India's rich culture and extensive history. It's central dome reaches an astounding 240 feet high with smaller domes surrounding, and the white marble appears to change color in the daylight.[2] To avoid large crowds make sure to arrive at the Taj Mahal when the gates open. If you happen to arrive in India during a full moon, the Taj Mahal is open for night tours (be sure to book ahead as there are limited spots available!).

Behind-the-Scenes Snapshot: This was the first place Bertram and I scouted for season 1 of *The Amazing Race*. When we first set out to create the route, we liked the idea of including locations that were considered wonders of the world. The Taj Mahal is on the list of new wonders of the world, and this iconic location set the tone for our first season.

Address: Dharmapuri, Forest Colony, Tajganj, Agra, Uttar Pradesh 282001, India

How to get there: Fly into Indira Gandhi International Airport in Delhi and take a train to Agra. There are over one hundred trains weekly and the journey takes three to four hours. From the train station take a taxi to the Taj Mahal.

☐ View the Taj Mahal from Mehtab Bagh
Season 27, Episode 9, Pit Stop

Just north of the Taj Mahal and across the Yamuna River is Mehtab Bagh, also known as the Moonlight Garden. This garden across the way is perfectly aligned with the Taj Mahal, and offers sweeping views of the beautiful monument. The garden actually predates the Taj Mahal by a hundred years, but it wasn't until Emperor Shah Jahan recognized it as the perfect place to view the Taj Mahal that he elevated the area, adding a pool, walkways, fountains, flowers, and even fruit trees. It was named the Moonlight Garden because at night the Taj Mahal is beautifully reflected in the pool and river.[3]

Address: Near Taj Mahal, Dharmapuri, Forest Colony, Agra, Uttar Pradesh 282001, India

Jaipur

☐ Visit the Amber Fort
Season 14, Episode 6, Roadblock

At the Amber Fort, one team member had to choose a group of camels and then bring the pack food and fill a trough of water for them. When finished, they received their next clue.

The Amber Fort was initially built in 1592 to act as a strong, safe haven against attacking enemies. The fort was completed by Mirja Raja Singh and is a representative mix of Hindu and Mughal styles. The exterior is harsh-looking, but this greatly contrasts with the beautiful white marble and sandstone interiors; visitors are often taken aback by the magnificent carvings, stones, and mirrors they begin to see on entering the fort.[4] Furthering its beauty, there are breathtaking views of Maota Lake in front. You can get to Amber Fort by walking up the hill, which takes about ten minutes, or if you're feeling more adventurous, you can also take a four-by-four to the top.[5]

Address: Devisinghpura, Amer, Jaipur, Rajasthan 302001, India

How to get there: You can fly into Jaipur, or you can take a train from another city. From Jaipur, take a bus, auto rickshaw, or taxi.

☐ *Go to the Top of Hawa Mahal*
Season 1, Episode 8, Detour

Teams traveled to Hawa Mahal, which was referred to as the "Palace of the Winds," to find their Detour.

Hawa Mahal is one of Jaipur's most distinctive landmarks. The Palace of the Winds is a pink-painted, "delicately honeycombed hive" that stands at five stories high.[6] The landmark was originally constructed in 1799, by Maharaja Sawai Pratap Singh, to allow women of the royal household to observe the happenings of life in the city (the building has 953 windows!). The top of the landmark offers sweeping views of the Jantar Mantar observatories and planetariums, the City Palace, and the Sireh Deori Bazaar. Hawa Mahal is said to be the tallest building without a foundation![7]

Address: Hawa Mahal Road, Badi Choupad, J.D.A. Market, Pink City, Jaipur, Rajasthan 302002, India

Delhi

☐ *Get a Ride in an Auto Rickshaw*
Season 1, Episode 7, Roadblock

One team member had to hire an auto rickshaw and find a shopkeeper on Maliwara Street in the congested Chandni Chowk Market who would show them a blue box containing a replica of the Taj Mahal with their next clue.

An auto rickshaw is a great way to get around in India. For easy on and off the vehicle lacks doors, and it can fit two comfortably (or three to four if you don't mind feeling crowded). Rickshaws are great for weaving in and out of congested traffic, and an inexpensive way to get around, but always negotiate a price ahead of time.

Behind-the-Scenes Snapshot: If you really want to know what it's like to live in a new place, it's so important to do the things the locals do. You have to step out of your comfort zone and into the streets and meet the people who live in the places you visit, or else you'll never truly experience the culture. This is why I love to travel, and why we had our contestants ride in an auto rickshaw.

Address: Chandni Chowk Market, 2573, Nai Sarak, Raghu Ganj, Roshanpura, Old Delhi, New Delhi, Delhi 110006, India

How to get there: From Indira Gandhi International Airport take the metro, bus, or hire a car into the city center.

Kolkata

☐ *Enjoy a Cup of Chai in the Tea Capital of India*

Season 18, Episode 6, Roadblock

At Kolkata Town Hall, one team member had to take part in an Indian tea tasting ceremony, searching among several hundred cups of tea to find the papaya- and mango-infused tea that they had tasted in a previous China task. When they found the correct cup of tea, they received their next clue.

Kolkata is considered the tea capital of India. There are many stalls on the famed Elgin Road that sell the finest teas in the city, served in a clay cup. When you order a cup of tea on Elgin Road, you can expect a theatrical experience; fires are lit, spices are crushed, sugar is added, and milk is poured from high heights.[8] When you finish your tea, the clay cup can be thrown into the street to be crushed by oncoming traffic (and it actually provides a handy solution to Kolkata's pothole problem!).[9]

Address: Kolkata Town Hall, Esplanade Row West, B.B.D. Bagh, Kolkata, West Bengal 700001, India

Address for Tea Shops: Elgin Road, Bhowanipore, Kolkata, West Bengal, India

How to get there: Fly into Netaji Subhas Chandra Bose International Airport in Kolkata, then take a bus, metro, or taxi.

☐ *Visit the Largest Flower Market in East India*

Season 5, Episode 9, Detour

Teams traveled to the Mallik Ghat Flower Market in Kolkata to find a particular stall and receive a garland, which they then had to release into the Ganges River for good luck and to receive their next clue.

If you're someone who enjoys exploring unconventional places, this can be counted as one of the most unique. The Mallik Ghat Flower Market was originally built in 1855 and is considered the biggest wholesale flower market in India and Asia![10] With doors opening at 4 a.m., this market is overflowing with vendors selling their flowers of different shapes, sizes, and colors. Some vendors live in makeshift shelters inside the market and work all hours making arrangements for special festivals or occasions. Since the market also supplies flowers to the neighboring states, packaging flowers in bales and transporting them is another significant activity here.[11]

Address: 68/3, Strand Bank Road, Fairley Place, B.B.D. Bagh, Kolkata, West Bengal 700001, India (southeast end of the Howrah Bridge)

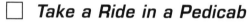

China

Beijing

☐ *Take a Ride in a Pedicab*

Season 1, Episode 11, Detour

Teams had to take three common forms of local transportation. First, teams had to travel by Bus 101 to Hujialou. Next, teams had to ride a motorcycle taxi to the Liu Jia Yao hotel. Finally, teams had to take a ride in a pedicab to Quan Xin Yuan Restaurant, where they would get their next clue.

The roads of Beijing are flooded with countless cars, so sometimes finding an alternative way to get around is more productive. Three-wheeled pedicabs are very popular and are usually at an advantage, as they can duck and weave through backstreets, avoiding traffic altogether. Their ability to disregard the rules and traffic might make you anxious, but they will get you where you need to go fast![12]

How to get there: Fly into Beijing Capital International Airport and take a taxi, bus, or train into the city center.

☐ *Visit the Great Wall of China*

Season 10, Episode 1, Pit Stop

At the Juyongguan section of the Great Wall of China, teams had to use a rope to scale the wall to reach the Pit Stop.

The Great Wall of China is one of the largest building projects that has ever been attempted. Built over two thousand years ago, the wall flows across northern China and into southern Mongolia for over thirteen thousand miles. The best-preserved part of the wall dates back to the Ming Dynasty (1368–1644) and spans close to fifty-five hundred miles.[13] Considered the most popular section of the wall, Juyongguan is the closest section to the main city of Beijing. Another popular stretch is the Mutianyu section, which is both traveler- and family-friendly.[14]

Behind-the-Scenes Snapshot: I had seen the Great Wall only in photographs and documentaries and tried to imagine what it would look like; when I finally did see it, it was far more beautiful and much grander than I had ever dreamed. It's difficult to comprehend that its construction began more than two thousand years ago and that it's more than thirteen thousand miles in length. It's truly a sight to be seen in person.

Address: Juyongguan Village, Nankou Town, Changping District, Beijing, China

How to get there: Take a taxi from Beijing.

☐ *Visit the Forbidden City*
Season 10, Episode 1, Route Marker

The Meridian Gate in the Forbidden City was the first leg's midpoint, where teams had to find a kiosk and select one of three departure times for the following morning. The last team to arrive at the kiosk was eliminated.

In the heart of Beijing is the Forbidden City, surrounded by gardens and temples. The Forbidden City was originally erected in 1406 by the Yongle Emperor of the Ming Dynasty, but it wasn't until 1420 that anyone occupied it.[15] The Forbidden City originally got its name from being an area that most people were barred from visiting; even the imperial family had limited access (the emperor was the only one allowed to enter whenever he pleased). The Forbidden City is the world's largest complex, expanding over 7.75 million square feet and separated from the city of Beijing by a 171-foot-wide moat and 33-foot-high wall.[16] As a visitor, you can explore the halls and courtyards and walk along the top of the 33-foot-high wall to take in the views!

Address: 4 Jingshan Front Street, Dongcheng, Beijing, China 100009
How to get there: Take a taxi from Beijing.

Xi'an

☐ Visit the Site
of the Terra-Cotta Warriors
Season 6, Episode 11, Route Marker

At the Museum of Qin Terra-Cotta Warriors and Horses, teams had to search for the clue box located on the viewing platform of Pit 1. The platform is raised and built around the largest pit, containing thousands of terra-cotta warriors and horses, which allows you to see the statues from a higher perspective.

The Terra-Cotta Warriors in Xi'an are one of the most famous archaeological finds in the world. The life-size army has stood guard over the soul of China's first emperor for more than two thousand years, but it wasn't until 1974 that they were discovered underground by local farmers digging for a well.[17] The farmers uncovered pieces of clay, which led to a full excavation, during which thousands of terra-cotta soldiers and horses were found in battle formation. Around eight thousand warriors (each with a unique face), one hundred chariots, four hundred horses, and more than one hundred thousand weapons have been discovered from the three existing pits so far.[18] The museum site is divided into three parts, in which one can view the three pits where ongoing reconstruction of the army is taking place.

Behind-the-Scenes Snapshot: It's wonderful to go to all the major cities of the world and see the tourist attractions, but it's also important to go beyond that and see places that are a bit off the beaten path. The site of the Terra-Cotta Warriors is one of those places. You cannot imagine the scope of this site and the detail of the work done by the artisans who built the warriors until you see it in person.

Address: The Museum of Qin Terra-Cotta Warriors and Horses, Qinling North Road, Lintong District, Xi'an, Shaanxi, China, 710600

How to get there: Fly into Xi'an Xianyang International Airport and take a taxi or bus. You can also take the bullet train from Beijing.

☐ *Take a Cable Car up Mount Hua and Place a Lock on the Railing at the Top*
Season 6, Episode 11, Roadblock

From the base of Mount Hua, teams had to travel by gondola to the North Peak. To get their next clue, one team member had to search among three thousand padlocks for the one that a provided key would unlock. Team members had to complete the Roadblock before the last gondola's departure time, at 7:00 p.m.

Located about an hour from Xi'an, Mount Hua has five main peaks: North, South, East, West, and Center. The North Peak is the lowest of the peaks at 5,295 feet, and the famous plank walk is located on the mountain's highest peak, the South, which has a height of 7,070 feet.[19] There are two cable cars to the top of Mount Hua—one to the North Peak, one to the West Peak. The elevation is so high and the paths are so steep that hiking can be incredibly tiring. At the top travelers can have their names engraved on a padlock and then attach it to one of the many railings. These padlocks are closed on the railing with wishes of good luck and health; couples will engrave their initials and attach their lock in hopes of being together forever.[20]

Address: Within Huayin, 714200 China

Hong Kong

☐ Ride the Hong Kong Tramway, Known Locally as the "Ding Ding"

Season 17, Episode 10, Detour

Teams had to ride the Hong Kong Tramway, a double-decker tram, also known as the "Ding Ding," between Arsenal Street and the Causeway Bay Tram Terminus, and look for three signs (reading "Pit Stop," "Statue," and "Square") that, when combined, would reveal the location of the Pit Stop.

Founded in 1904, the Hong Kong Tramways are the world's biggest double-decker tram system still operating. Carrying an average of two hundred thousand passengers every day, the ride is completely eco-friendly and electric, and runs the length of Hong Kong island (an eight-mile route).[21] The sound of the horn is where the "Ding Ding" nickname comes from, as the bell always rings twice.[22] The stations in Hong Kong are usually set on "islands," with stops existing in the middle of the street. Make sure to board through the rear door, and exit in the front (you will pay on your way out!).

How to get there: Fly into Hong Kong International Airport and take a taxi, bus, train, or rent a car.

☐ *Get Your Picture Taken at Victoria Peak*
Season 30, Episode 11, Route Marker

Upon arrival in Hong Kong, teams traveled to Victoria Peak, where they had their picture taken with the Hong Kong skyline as the backdrop. After it was printed, teams were given the photograph and their next clue.

Victoria Peak is the highest point on the island of Hong Kong, standing at 1,811 feet tall. This historic mountain boasts 360-degree views of Hong Kong Harbor and the city's skyline. There are several different lookout points and hiking trails on the peak (if you're looking to get away from the crowds). If it's a nice day, you can choose to hike to the peak, but if that is not your thing, you can take a taxi to the top, or you can take the Peak Tram; the tram opened in 1888 and is among the world's oldest funiculars![23]

Address: Peak Tram Lower Terminus, 33 Garden Road, Central, Hong Kong, China

South Korea

Seoul

☐ *Take a Taekwondo Class*
Season 4, Episode 10, Detour

Teams used a map to find a marked Taekwondo *dojang* where each team member had to break three sets of wooden boards to receive their clue.

Taekwondo is the most recognized form of Korean martial arts; it emphasizes a sense of morality, humility, and respect for one's opponent. It's a sport that can help you not only improve physically but improve mentally as well.[24] This form of martial arts teaches the subject offensive tactics but specifically focuses on defensive techniques, because of the Taekwondo spirit of respecting peace and justice.[25] You can take a one-day class in Seoul and experience this traditional Korean martial art yourself.

How to get there: Fly into Incheon International Airport and take the metro, bus, train, taxi, or rent a car.

☐ *Go White-Water Rafting down the Hantan River*
Season 17, Episode 11, Route Marker

Upon arrival in Seoul, teams had to drive toward North Korea, to the Seungil Bridge in the Korean Demilitarized Zone. There, they had to white-water raft down the Hantan River and board a Humvee that took them to Camp Casey in Dongducheon, where the next clue was located.

The Hantan River area is considered to be the best place to raft or kayak in South Korea. Situated about an hour outside Seoul, this area is very scenic (some even refer to it as the Grand Canyon of Korea); you definitely will enjoy the awe-inspiring views you'll take in while moving down the river. The river is also known for its unique Giamgoeseok rock formations, so you can ask your guide about any rock or cliff jumping along the way.[26] Rafting season runs from mid-April through October.

☐ *Learn How to Make Kimchi*
Season 29, Episode 11, Route Marker

At Mugyewon Arts & Cultural Center, teams had to prepare the traditional dish kimchi after watching a demonstration. Once it was approved, they had to transfer it to a jar and then bury the closed jar in soil to start fermentation. Lastly, after tasting some kimchi, teams received their next clue.

If you want to connect with South Korean culture, kimchi is a sure-fire way to make that happen. The spicy, fermented side dish is often consumed with every meal in South Korea, and with over one hundred different types, you can find it on every corner. It's said that the average Korean eats around forty-eight pints of kimchi per year.[27] You should definitely try it on your trip, but if you want to take it a step further, a great way to learn about kimchi is by making it. There are many cooking classes across the city that will show you how you can make your own recipe or follow more traditional instructions. One of the most popular locations is the Seoul Kimchi Academy, which offers many classes led by professional chefs. You will follow instructions to make it, taste your handmade kimchi, and have it packed up so that you can take it home with you![28]

Address: Mugyewon Arts & Cultural Center, 03022 2, Changuimun-ro 5ga-gil, Jongno-gu, Seoul

Tokyo

☐ **Stay in a Capsule Hotel**

Season 9, Episode 11, Route Marker

At Capsule Land Hotel, the final three teams checked in for an overnight rest and were given one of three departure times fifteen minutes apart depending on their arrival. Upon departure, they received their clue, which told the teams to drive their car to Fuji-Q Highland in Fujiyoshida to find their next clue.

There's truly nothing like it. Individual pods in the wall, sometimes dozens to a room, with a bed, a light to illuminate your single pod, and maybe a TV. Native to Japan, you can find capsule hotels all over the country. Some will remind you of creepy sci-fi movies, while others are comfortable small sleeping rooms with windows and views. Each hotel "room" will oftentimes be only as wide and long as a single bed (and about that tall).[29] Make sure you aren't claustrophobic before booking a room at a capsule hotel—if tight spaces don't bother you, you won't find a better place to sleep at such a reasonable price!

How to get there: Fly into Haneda International Airport and take a train, bus, or taxi.

☐ *Cross the Shibuya Scramble Intersection*

Season 9, Episode 11, Route Marker

Teams drove through the streets of Tokyo to the Sakamoto Building in Shibuya. They then walked to the Shibuya Scramble Crossing and scanned the big flashing video billboards to find their next clue: "Find Hachiko!"

The Shibuya Intersection is considered the world's busiest crosswalk intersection. Miraculously, with people walking in all different directions, pedestrians manage to avoid running into one another (and the crossing often has around a thousand people crossing at a time).[30] With ten lanes of traffic and five major crosswalks converging, the controlled chaos of Shibuya's "Scramble" demonstrates the drive and focus of this cutting-edge city. Step into the action, take a walk on the wild side, cross the intersection with thousands, and be sure to stop in front of the Shibuya train station. Here you can visit the statue of Hachiko, the loyal Akita dog who is a hero to the Japanese people. He would wait for his owner at the station every day in the 1920s. When his owner died unexpectedly, Hachiko continued to visit the station every day for the next ten years.[31] His statue is a very popular place for locals and tourists looking to take pictures with him and to honor the noble dog. Even the buses and vending machines in the area have Hachiko's face on them, and there's a mascot that frequents the area.[32]

Address: 1 Chome-2-1 Dogenzaka, Shibuya City, Tokyo 150-0043, Japan

Tokyo and Nagano

☐ Take a Bullet Train to Nagano and Skate on the Olympic Track
Season 26, Episode 2, Detour

In this Detour, teams had to ride a bullet train 150 miles from Tokyo to Nagano and make their way to the M-Wave Olympic Arena. Each team member had to sit in a chair mounted on a sled while their partner pushed the chair around the speed skating track for one lap, and then the two of them would trade places. When they were able to finish both laps under three minutes and fifty-five seconds, they received their next clue.

Japan's bullet trains are called Shinkansen. You can purchase a Japan Rail Pass to easily travel to Nagano from Japan's major cities. The trains can reach a top speed of 199 mph, and the trip from Tokyo to Nagano takes approximately one and a half hours.[33] The M-Wave is a covered speed skating oval that was constructed for the 1998 Winter Olympics. The arena was also the location of the opening and closing ceremonies. From October to March, you can skate on the famed ice, and from April through September, the arena is a great place to see a concert![34]

Address: 195 Kitanagaike, Nagano, 381-0025, Japan

How to get there: Take the bullet train from Tokyo and then take a taxi.

Hanoi

☐ *Visit Hỏa Lò Prison, Where John McCain Was Kept Prisoner*

Season 10, Episode 3, Route Marker

At the Hỏa Lò Prison museum, teams had to search the grounds to find a room with John McCain's flight suit in it to receive their next clue.

Tortured and held captive as a prisoner of the North Vietnamese for five and a half years during the Vietnam War, the man who later became Senator John McCain is etched into Hanoi's history forever. A memorial stands at the lake where his plane crashed, and the prison where he was held captive is now a museum.[35] The museum displays McCain's flight suit and parachute, and many of the prison cells have been well preserved. A visit to the museum is both powerful and difficult. When Senator McCain passed away in 2018, Hanoi residents held a memorial for him at the lake, leaving flowers "to remember the man who fought for peace in many countries, including Vietnam."[36]

Address: 1 Hoa Lo Street Hoan Kiem, Hanoi 10000 Vietnam

How to get there: Fly into Nội Bài International Airport in Hanoi and take a taxi.

☐ *Prepare Vietnam's National Dish, Phở, in a Cooking Class*

Season 22, Episode 5, Detour

Teams had to prepare Vietnam's national dish, *phở*, by first getting four baskets at Ngọc Sơn Temple, and then navigating through a street market to find ingredients from a shopping list. After acquiring the ingredients, teams had to find a cooking station and cook *phở* soup to the chef's approval to receive their next clue.

The *phở* that is so popular in Vietnam is a soup that consists of beef-bone broth, herbs, bean sprouts, rice noodles, and thinly sliced beef or chicken. Find a cooking class where you can learn how to make different types of *phở*, as there are variations from North and South Vietnam and you should find which you like best.

Ha Long Bay

☐ *Take a Local Boat Called a Sampan*

Season 10, Episode 4, Detour

For both Detour options, teams had to row a sampan to their task. In "Over," they had to row to a ship in the bay and load supplies onto the sampan, then row to a floating village to deliver goods to the specific addresses on their invoice. When finished, teams rowed back to the provisions ship and presented the finished invoice to the captain, who would give them their next clue. In "Under," teams had to row the sampan to a marked buoy at a pearl farm, where they had to haul thirty baskets out of the sea and into their boats. They had to deliver the baskets to a pearl farmer to receive their next clue.

Ha Long Bay is a natural wonder in Vietnam consisting of more than sixteen hundred islands and inlets. Beautiful beaches, natural limestone caves, and floating villages are a must-see, and doing so by boat is the best way to get close to the action.[37] On the waters of Ha Long Bay, you will see two different types of sampans—the traditional and the long-canoe style (this one is used for faster transport to and from the bay's floating fishing villages).[38]

How to get there: Take a train or bus from Hanoi.

☐ *Take a Cruise on a Junk*
Season 10, Episode 4, Detour

For both Detour options, teams were taken on a junk to a location near the Detour, then given a junk to row to their task in Ha Long Bay.

A junk is a classic Chinese sailing vessel, and while some are nicer than others, all are impressive, with their curved sails and decorative wood carvings. The most popular way to experience Ha Long Bay is by taking an overnight junk cruise; you can choose the duration of your voyage in advance. Many of the modern junk boats are spacious and luxurious, with deck space to enjoy the phenomenal views.[39]

Ho Chi Minh City

☐ See a Golden Dragon Water Puppet Theater Show
Season 15, Episode 3, Route Marker

At the start of the leg, teams had to travel to the Golden Dragon Water Puppet Theater. There, they had to grab an *Amazing Race*–colored ribbon from the mouth of a dragon puppet moving about in the water. Inside the ribbon was a small metal capsule with a postage stamp concealed inside, leaving teams to figure out that the stamp depicted the Saigon Central Post Office (referred to as the "Ho Chi Minh City Post Office" in the show), where they would find their next clue.

For generations, puppeteers in Vietnam have put on shows in waist-deep water. Water puppetry theaters (like the Golden Dragon Water Puppet Theater) continue this Vietnamese tradition in a modern, family-friendly way. Water puppet shows are often associated with the people of Vietnam and the lives they live spiritually. These shows are performed on the surface of a water pool, with the puppeteers holding their puppets using long bamboo rods and strings under the water.[40] Oftentimes an orchestra will accompany the show, with the puppets acting out the songs. The Golden Dragon is Saigon's main water-puppet venue, with two shows each night.

Address: 55B Nguyễn Thị Minh Khai, Phường Bến Thành, Quận 1, Thành phố Ho Chi Minh, Vietnam

How to get there: Fly into Tan Sơn Nhat International Airport and take a taxi or bus.

☐ Go to Reunification Palace, the Site of the End of the Vietnam War

Season 15, Episode 3, Pit Stop

Originally designed as a home for former president Ngo Dinh Diem, this building is most notable for being the place where Saigon fell in April 1975, when North Vietnamese tanks broke down the gates and their flag was hung on the balcony to claim victory.[41] The "very tanks that crashed through the gates are enshrined in the entryway, and photos and accounts of their drivers are on display."[42] As a visitor you can tour the private bedrooms, dining rooms, and more. Make sure to take a look at the war command room, with its huge maps and old communication equipment, as well as the basement, where ongoing screenings of war propaganda films are shown in different rooms.

Address: 135 Nam Ky Khoi Nghia Street, District 1, Ho Chi Minh City, Vietnam

☐ Experience Skiing and Sledding Indoors at Snow Town Saigon

Season 31, Episode 4, Route Marker

At Snow Town Saigon, teams had to grab a sled and ride it down an indoor slope to a person dressed as a polar bear, who would give them their next clue.

Inside Snow Town, it will feel as if you're walking through a winter town in Europe! You can experience fun winter activities such as sledding and snowman making, or even try skiing down the twenty-six-foot hill! The fluffy snow is made with state-of-the-art snow-making technology from Japan, and you can enjoy it all right in the heart of Saigon.[43]

Address: 125 Dong Van Cong Street, Thành My Loi Ward, District 2, Ho Chi Minh City, Vietnam

Thailand

Chiang Mai

☐ ## Explore Royal Park Ratchaphruek
Season 30, Episode 10, Route Marker

After arriving in Chiang Mai, teams had to search the grounds of Royal Park Ratchaphruek for elephant statues. Here they would find red and yellow garlands that had to be delivered to one of four ladies holding umbrellas in the park.

The Royal Park Ratchaphruek was originally built to celebrate the sixtieth anniversary of King Bhumibol Adulyadej's accession to the throne, as well as his eightieth birthday.[44] It has become one of the most popular ecotourism places in Chiang Mai, and is considered a center of agricultural research. The large floral and botanical park has immeasurable plants and flowers, including gorgeous orchid gardens. The international gardens are modeled after the World Expo, with each garden representing the flora of a particular nation from around the world; each garden is an experiment to see how that nation's native plant will grow in Thailand.[45] The gardens are so vast that you can either walk, rent a bike, hire a golf cart, or take a tram around the grounds. And make sure to check out the temple—it's a bit of a climb but definitely worth it.

Address: 334 Mae Hia, Mueang Chiang Mai District, Chiang Mai 50100, Thailand

How to get there: Fly into Chiang Mai International Airport and take a bus, taxi, or tuk-tuk to the city center.

Bangkok

☐ Visit the Temple of the Reclining Buddha

Season 1, Episode 9, Fast Forward

This Fast Forward required teams to travel to the Temple of the Reclining Buddha and play a game that used the 108 bronze urns set alongside the giant Buddha. They had to choose a bowl of coins and drop exactly one coin into every bronze urn. If the bowl a team chose had too little or too many coins, they had to choose another bowl to play again. The first team to find the bowl with exactly 108 coins would win the Fast Forward.

The Temple of the Reclining Buddha, also known as Wat Pho, is a very famous Buddhist temple known for its almost 50-foot-long, 150-foot-high Buddha covered in gold leaf. This is the largest reclining Buddha statue in Thailand, but there are many more reclining Buddhas all over the country—there are even 394 other such Buddhas in this particular complex![46] You can hire a tour guide to take you around the temple, and once you're done walking around, you can get a traditional Thai massage right on the grounds. Like the contestants on *The Amazing Race*, you too can put coins in the 108 bowls and make a wish. Even if your wish doesn't come true, the money goes to a good cause, helping the monks to maintain the beautiful appearance of Wat Pho.[47]

Address: 2 Sanamchai Road, Phra Borom Maha Ratchawang, Phra Nakhon, Bangkok 10200, Thailand

How to get there: Fly into Suvarnabhumi Airport and take the train into the city center or rent a car.

☐ Take a Long-Tail Boat on the Waterways to See the City
Season 14, Episode 8, Roadblock

One team member had to properly attach a propeller to a traditional Thai long-tail boat in order to receive the next clue. After the Roadblock, teams had to navigate the waterways of Bangkok in their long-tail boat using a provided map to find the Peninsula Pier for the next clue.

Getting around Bangkok by boat is a popular option among travelers and locals, who navigate the busy network of canals on a daily basis. Long-tail boats are like taxis on the water (and can be rented privately); you can also hop on a busy boat with stops along the way, visiting local food vendors or people selling trinkets. You may want to book a tour with a guide who can share insights about the areas you will see and give you a greater understanding of life on the river.[48]

Rent a boat or book a tour with the many vendor options in Bangkok. Make sure to choose one that takes you to places you're excited to see!

☐ *Play Snooker at a Snooker Club*
Season 26, Episode 4, Detour

Teams traveled to Sathon Road in central Bangkok and then took a tuk-tuk to the Snooker Club. Once there, they played snooker until they sank a red ball, at which point they were given a bottle of milk marked only with a logo. They then had to find the Caturday Cat Café elsewhere in Bangkok and feed the milk to the resident cats to receive their next clue.

Snooker, a British billiards game very similar to American billiards (pool), is played with twenty-two balls, with each player trying to pocket first the red and then the non-red balls, scoring one point per red ball and the number value of the others. It's thought that the game was invented in India in the 1870s as a game for soldiers.[49] There are countless snooker halls in Bangkok, with a very popular one being Hi-End Snooker Club, a world-class facility that hosted the 2019 World Women's Snooker Championship.[50]

The Caturday Cat Café is a cat lover's dream and is the perfect place to hang out and enjoy a refreshment while more than thirty pampered resident cats freely roam around the room and lounge. The café is decorated in all things cats, and there are even decorations that come off the wall for you to use to play with the feline friends![51]

Address: Hi-End Snooker Club, 17/730 Wang Hin Condominium Lardpraw-Wanghin Road, Bangkok 10230, Thailand

Address: Caturday Cat Café, 89/35 Phayathai Rd., Khwaeng Thanon Phetchaburi, Khet Ratchathewi, Krung Thep Maha Nakhon 10400, Thailand

☐ Eat a One-Thousand-Year-Old Egg from the Wat Klang Food Market
Season 26, Episode 4, Detour

Teams traveled on foot to Sathorn Pier and then took a water taxi to Wat Intharam Pier, where they searched for the Wat Klang Food Market. At the market, each team member had to eat a thousand-year-old egg. Then they received a metal placard clue sending them to the Wat Paknam Bhasicharoen temple to participate in a traditional Thai prayer before receiving their next clue.

Located in Bangkok's Old Quarter, Wat Klang Market is the city's best daytime street food market. The mazelike market is full of shops selling clothing, accessories, and of course, street food. A century egg (also called a thousand-year-old egg) is a Chinese delicacy. It's a duck egg (but can sometimes be a hen or quail egg) that goes through a very specific fermentation process. The egg is submerged in a mixture of salt, water, coal, and calcium oxide for one hundred days. During this time, the shell completely dissolves, the white part of the egg turns into an amber jelly, and the yolk turns green

> OTHER BANGKOK MUST-SEES!
>
> - GRAND PALACE
> - GIANT SWING
> - CHATUCHAK MARKET
> - DAMNOEN SADUAK FLOATING MARKET

(resembling mold).[52] The egg tastes a bit like a strong, smelly cheese, the smell mixed with that of ammonia. Definitely a once-in-a-lifetime experience!

Address: Wat Klang Food Market, close to Wat Intharam Pier, 258 Bang Yi Ruea, Thon Buri, Bangkok 10600, Thailand

(Near) Yogyakarta

☐ ### *Descend 160 Feet into Jomblang Cave (Goa Jomblang)*

Season 19, Episode 2, Roadblock

One team member had to descend 160 feet into Goa Jomblang to search for a traditional Javanese mask and a dagger. Once they located them, team members had to scale a bamboo ladder before delivering the items to a local chieftain in exchange for their next clue.

Jomblang Cave is a collapsed sinkhole that is part of a cave system just outside Yogyakarta. Cave-goers are lowered by staff 165 feet on a rope. Once they reach the bottom, visitors can hike down a tunnel to Grubug Cave.[53] Basic tickets for the cave are on a first come, first served basis. These tickets include safety gear and the help of workers to lower you down into the cave. You can also book a tour of the cave, which will include admission.

Address: Jetis, Pacarejo, Semanu, Gunung Kidul Regency, Special Region of Yogyakarta 55893, Indonesia

How to get there: Fly into Yogyakarta International Airport and take a taxi, hire a car, or rent a car.

Java

☐ *Explore the Largest Buddhist Temple in the World*
Season 19, Episode 3, Roadblock

One racer had to walk around the top tier of the Borobudur temple, counting the statues of the Five Dhyani Buddhas, while also paying attention to the mudra depicted by each of the statues. Mudras are symbolic hand gestures, and to receive their next clue the team member had to demonstrate the gestures and also give the correct number of Buddhas to the local at the base of the temple.

The Borobudur temple, located on the island of Java, is considered the world's largest Buddhist monument. Built in the ninth century, the temple sits on the top of a hill and overlooks fields and other, distant hills. The monument is very large in square feet, measuring 403 feet by 403 feet at the base.[54] Even after ten centuries of neglect, and though it was built without the use of cement or mortar, the temple has remained strong. It's unknown when a volcano erupted and covered the temple in volcanic ash, but the structure was rediscovered in 1815 buried under the ash. In the 1970s, the Indonesian government and UNESCO worked to restore Borobudur to its original glory. The restoration took about eight years to complete, and today the temple is a valuable treasure to Indonesia and the world.[55]

Address: Jl. Badrawati, Kw. Candi Borobudur, Borobudur, Kec. Borobudur, Magelang, Jawa Tengah, Indonesia

OCEANIA

Australia

Sydney

☐ Visit Harry's Café de Wheels and Eat an Entire Meat Pie

Season 2, Episode 9, Fast Forward

The Fast Forward required one team to go to Harry's Café de Wheels, where each team member had to eat a meat pie to win the award.

Harry's Café de Wheels has been operating for more than eighty years, serving people like Frank Sinatra, Sir Elton John, and Prince Harry their iconic "Tiger" pie. The Tiger pie, a signature creation of Harry's Café de Wheels, is a meat pie topped with mashed potatoes, peas, and a sizable serving of gravy. The original founder, Harry "Tiger" Edwards, established the restaurant when failing to find a late-night snack that fit his needs; the caravan café is near the front gates of Woolloomooloo naval dockyard in Sydney, Australia.[1]

Address: Cowper Wharf Road & Dowling Street, Woolloomooloo NSW 2011, Australia

How to get there: Fly into Sydney Kingsford Smith Airport and take the train, taxi, or rent a car.

☐ *Climb the Sydney Harbour Bridge*
Season 2, Episode 9, Route Marker

At the start of the leg, teams traveled to find BridgeClimb Sydney and sign up for a climb to the top of the Sydney Harbour Bridge to obtain the next clue.

The famous BridgeClimb Sydney has been around since 1998, offering visitors the ability to scale to the summit of the nationally adored Sydney Harbour Bridge. Climbing to take in the awe-inspiring 360-degree views is available at dawn, during the day, at twilight, and even at night! To date, almost 4 million locals and visitors have climbed the bridge, and some even chose to spend their important life moments there; the bridge has been the stage for more than five thousand proposals and over thirty weddings. The Sydney Harbour Bridge remains the most climbed bridge globally, and has been voted the #1 Experience in Australia.[2] Check it out!

Address: 3 Cumberland Street, The Rocks NSW 2000, Australia

☐ *Walk Through Hyde Park*
Season 2, Episode 8, Roadblock

One team member had to follow a series of clues written in Australian slang. First, they had to take a bus to a surfie (surfer) in the lairy daks (flashy, colorful shorts) at Martin Place and say "g'day, mate." Then they had to find a true-blue ankle biter (child) riding a bicycle around Archibald Fountain in Hyde Park, and then a sheila (woman) in an Aussie cozzie (swim suit) near the Captain Cook Statue in Hyde Park, whom they should ask for "the good oil" (useful information). And then they had to find a bushie (country person who resides in the Australian Outback) in the Circular Quay. Team members continued this task until they received a clue instructing them to reunite with their partner.

Hyde Park is both the oldest and most well-known park in Australia. The park offers thirty-nine and a half acres of wide-open space and around 580 exotic and native trees.[3] There are many festivals and events that take place in the park every year, including the Sydney Festival, the Food and Wine Fair, and Australia Day. A popular spot for visitors and locals alike, Hyde Park offers a beautiful central park in the middle of Sydney.

Address: Elizabeth Street, Sydney NSW 2000, Australia

☐ *Visit the Sydney Opera House*
Season 2, Episode 8, Route Marker

Upon arrival in Sydney, teams made their way to the steps of the famous Sydney Opera House to get their next clue.

In 1947, the opera conductor of the Sydney Symphony Orchestra identified the need for a music facility to house concerts and theatrical productions; after many years and a design competition to determine the outside architecture, the Sydney Opera House opened in 1973. The beauty of the facility is unlike any other, with its unique use of a series of white sail-shaped shells as its roof structure making it one of the most photographed buildings in the world.[4] As Australia's number one tourist destination and busi-

> OTHER SYDNEY MUST-SEES!
>
> · BONDI BEACH
> · LUNA PARK
> · CATCH A MATCH OF AUSSIE FOOTBALL
> · HARBOR CRUISE FROM CIRCULAR QUAY
> · SYDNEY TOWER
> · ROYAL BOTANICAL GARDENS

est performing arts center, the 2,679-seat Concert Hall has hosted more than 1,800 performances and more than 1.4 million people, through concerts, choir performances, popular music shows, operas, and dance performances. The site alone welcomes more than 10.9 million visitors a year.[5]

Address: Bennelong Point, Sydney NSW 2000, Australia

Coober Pedy

☐ Mine for Opal
at Tom's Working Opal Mine

Season 2, Episode 9, Detour

Teams had to find the Opal Quest Mine at Tom's Working Opal Mine. Once at the mining company, teams headed down into the cool tunnels and, using traditional mining tools, searched within a large pile of dirt that hid an opal. After finding an "opal," they returned to the surface to show the judge what they'd found and collect the next clue.

Tom's Working Opal Mine is a modern-day mine in the Stone Field of Coober Pedy, South Australia. Open daily, the mine welcomes visitors of all ages who are looking to experience the way opal mining is conducted today. Experienced miners and guides provide explanations while you try various mining features, shovel sandstone, jack-pick on a level, learn about the explosives necessary for mining (and how to stay safe), and see the "Tunneling Machine."[6] The mine is safe, spacious, well lit, and easy to walk through; there's no crouching through narrow tunnels, and the facility is wheelchair friendly.

Address: Lot 1993 Stuart Highway, Coober Pedy SA 5723, Australia

How to get there: Fly from Sydney Kingsford Smith Airport to Coober Pedy Airport and take a taxi.

☐ *Play Golf on the Driest Golf Course in the World*

Season 2, Episode 9, Detour

Teams played three holes of golf on the driest golf course in the world, Coober Pedy Opal Fields Golf Club. Using a piece of Astroturf to tee off at each hole, as the course is all dirt, teams had to play in the intense heat of up to 130°F to receive their clue.

Appearing in various Top 10 lists for most unusual golf courses in the world, the Coober Pedy Opal Fields Golf Club has been offering a unique course for golfers since 1976.[7] Across the desert flats of Coober Pedy, golfers are given a piece of artificial grass to allow them to tee off, as well as three gold balls (it's very easy to lose them when they're constantly bouncing off rocks). The golf course, in "the impossible to irrigate outback," is the only course in the world (and in six hundred years) to be granted reciprocal playing rights for their members at the famous St Andrews course in Scotland.[8] A game at the course will only set you back $20 a round, and any opal you find during the game is yours to keep!

Behind-the-Scenes Snapshot: This place, in the center of Australia, is what it must look like on the moon! The hotel we stayed in while filming was literally underground. Due to the extreme summer heat—there are no trees here, and temperatures can reach nearly 130 degrees Fahrenheit—it's simply the best solution. I remember flying into Coober Pedy in a tiny airplane carrying five people and thinking that if anything happened to the pilot, we would have no one to land the plane! It was then that I decided to take flying lessons as soon as I was back home.

Address: LOT 1509 Rowe Drive, Coober Pedy SA 5723, Australia

Season 30. Twins Eric and Daniel travel with the Travelocity Roaming Gnome to receive their next clue in Tangiers, Morocco.

Image Credit: ViacomCBS

Season 3. In Marrakech, teams rode quad bikes in the Palmeraie Oasis in search of their next clue.

Image Credit: ViacomCBS

Season 5. In Luxor, Egypt, teams crossed the Nile in a felucca, a traditional Egyptian sailboat.

Image Credit: Sally Bedding >

Season 22. Giraffes spotted in Tanzania.

< Image Credit: ViacomCBS

Season 31. In Dubai, Phil stands at the base of the 2,722-foot Burj Khalifa, the tallest building in the world since its completion in 2010.

Image Credit: ViacomCBS

Season 5. Chip and Kim ride camels across the Dubai desert to their next Pit Stop.

Image Credit: ViacomCBS

Season 5. In Dubai, teams had to tandem skydive from ten thousand feet into the Margham Desert.

Image Credit: ViacomCBS

Season 15. At the Dubai Autodrome, one team member
had to drive a single lap around the track
in forty-five seconds.

Season 14. Teams had to attach a propeller to
a traditional long-tail boat in Bangkok, Thailand.

Season 9. In Tokyo, Japan, teams sleep for
the night at the Capsule Land Hotel.

Image Credit: ViacomCBS

Season 10. In Ha Long Bay, Vietnam, a junk
sets the scene for this leg of the race.

Image Credit: Chad Baron

Season 27. Mehtab Bagh, overlooking the Taj Mahal in Agra, India, served as the backdrop for this Pit Stop.

Image Credit: ViacomCBS

Season 7. In Lucknow, India, teams search for their next clue at the Bara Imambara monument.

Image Credit: ViacomCBS

Season 6. In Mount Hua, China, Hayden and Rebecca search hundreds of locks to find the one that fits their individual key.

Image Credit: ViacomCBS

Season 10. Teams had to climb the Juyongguan section of the Great Wall of China to reach the Pit Stop.

Image Credit: ViacomCBS

Season 30. In this task, teammates Cody and Jessica went to Victoria Peak to have their picture taken overlooking the Hong Kong skyline.

Image Credit: ViacomCBS

Season 9. Wat Ben-chamabophit Buddhist temple in Bangkok, Thailand, was the Pit Stop for this leg of the race.

< Image Credit: Elise Doganieri

Season 2. The rooftop of the Museum of Contemporary Art, overlooking Sydney Harbour and the Sydney Harbor Bridge, was the Pit Stop in Sydney, Australia.

Image Credit: ViacomCBS >

Auckland

☐ *Climb the Auckland Harbour Bridge*
Season 5, Episode 11, Roadblock

For this Roadblock, one team member had to travel by boat to the Auckland Harbour Bridge and climb a seventy-five-foot ladder to the girders beneath the roadway. From there, they had to walk along the girders until they retrieved the clue on the other side.

One of Auckland's most recognizable landmarks is now a playground for adventure. The fully guided tour takes you to the top of the bridge and allows you to see the awe-inspiring views, all on custom-engineered, safe walkways.[9] This unforgettable adventure takes climbers under, around, up, and over the historic bridge. The last of its kind to be built in the world, this suspension bridge has three thousand berths and is the largest in the southern hemisphere.[10] Not only can you climb to the top of the Auckland Harbour Bridge but you can also jump from it attached to a bungee cord.

Address: 105 Curran Street Extension, Westhaven Marina, Herne Bay, Auckland, New Zealand

How to get there: Fly into Auckland Airport and rent a car or take a taxi.

☐ *Ride Around in a Blokart*
Season 13, Episode 4, Detour

For the detour, teams had to assemble two Blokarts, and each team member had to complete three laps around a track to receive their next clue from the track official.

A Blokart, also known as a "land yacht," is a small, easy-to-maneuver go-kart with an attached sail. Driving a Blokart does not require previous sailing experience and allows beginners the opportunity to experience sailing on land, but Blokarting is also a competitive sport for those who train.[11] Many local companies offer lessons and open hours so you can experience the thrill of Blokarting.

How to get there: Fly into Auckland Airport and rent a car. You can also transfer at Auckland Airport and fly into Tauranga Airport and rent a car or take a taxi from there.

Waitomo District

☐ *Go Spelunking at the Waitomo Caves*
Season 2, Episode 11, Detour

The Detour was a choice between "Drop" and "Climb." In Drop, teams had to descend 325 feet into a cavern known as "The Lost World" and then walk a short distance to Jesus Rock to receive the next clue. In Climb, teams had to climb down a one-hundred-foot ladder into the same cavern, then walk a much longer distance to reach the next clue.

Rappel 325 feet down into Waitomo Caves' "The Lost World" and explore the massive cave vaults below. The descent takes about twenty minutes, but you will lower yourself down beside your instructor, who can give you information and reassurance, so no need to be nervous! The walls of the cave as you descend are covered in lush greenery, and when you reach the ground, you can enjoy the awe-inspiring views from the bottom. Once you get your footing, you're taken through the underground caves, and when you turn off your headlamp, you will be able to take in the beauty of the glow worms around you. Glow worms are a big reason why people come to Waitomo, as visitors will often embark on glow worm excursions in the area.[12] When you're done exploring, you climb rocks and a series of ladders to once again stand on the surface.

Address: 1227 Waitomo Valley Road, Waitomo Caves 3977, New Zealand

How to get there: Fly into Auckland Airport and rent a car or take a taxi or bus.

Rotorua District

☐ Run down the Mouth of a Dormant Volcano
Season 2, Episode 11, Fast Forward

One team had to perform a "scree run" down Mount Tarawera, a run down the loose rock walls directly into the mouth of the dormant volcano, to obtain the Fast Forward reward.

The eruption of Mount Tarawera in 1886 was one of New Zealand's worst recorded disasters. Villages were devastated, the famous Pink and White Terraces were destroyed, and 120 people perished. The volcanic crater is now safe to climb, though you must be with a tour guide, as Mount Tarawera is on sacred land.[13] The three peaks and six craters allow for 360-degree views, and all from 3,645 feet. A scree run is described as running and jumping down a steep slope into a volcanic crater. Make sure to slam your heels into the sand to keep upright and avoid tumbling down. The walk itself is about two and a half miles long and the loop takes approximately two hours to complete.[14]

Behind-the-Scenes Snapshot: I had never done anything like this before, and it's such a fun memory. As you run down the volcanic rocks into the crater, you almost feel weightless; it might have been the speed at which I was going (which was fast), but you pick up so much momentum as you run downhill that you feel like you're walking on the moon! As your feet sink just a bit into the loose rock, you also propel yourself forward. It's truly a unique experience!

☐ *Go River Sledging on the Kaituna River*

Season 5, Episode 10, Detour

Teams had to drive thirteen miles to Okere Falls to put on protective gear and perform an adventure sport called river sledging on the Kaituna River. With the help of the two guides, teams had to complete a one-mile course with only a small board, called a sledge. At the end of the course, the instructor gave them their next clue.

The first water sledge was built in New Zealand in 1981, and the sport is now a professional one in Europe. River sledging is best described as white-water rafting mixed with luge. You will shoot down a river clinging to a board, all while coming in contact with grade-three rapids. Instead of just floating down the river, you will be stopped by the guide at each rapid and instructed on the best way to proceed.[15] Sledging on the Kaituna River is considered more extreme, so it's recommended that you be a strong swimmer and confident in water.[16]

☐ *Enjoy a Soothing Geothermal Mud Bath*
Season 5, Episode 10, Detour

Teams had to travel ten miles to Hell's Gate and search within the marked area of a bubbling hot mud pit for their next clue.

Since 1871, Tikitere has been a destination for spa and nature lovers because of its beauty and healing properties. In 1934, Irish playwright George Bernard Shaw visited, and in awe of the boiling mud and steam he exclaimed "This could be the very gates of hell."[17] When local people heard this, they decided the English name for Tikitere would become "Hell's Gate." The geothermal mud-and-sulphur mineral water here has been used for over eight hundred years because of its healing properties and body and soul revitalization. Because of the geothermal activity in this area, the nutrient-rich soil and perfect temperatures give life to trees like the silver fern and rare mosses you won't find elsewhere.[18]

Address: 351 State Highway 30, Tikitere, Rotorua 3010, New Zealand

Queenstown

☐ ***Bungee Jump off
the Nevis Highwire Platform***
Season 2, Episode 10, Detour

At Wentworth Station, teams found marked four-by-four vehicles parked on the side of the road. They instructed the driver of their four-by-four to take them to the gondola. Two teams at a time took a gondola across this massive gorge to the Nevis Highwire Platform. Teams then had to take a tandem bungee jump nearly 440 feet, the second-highest bungee jump in the world at the time. Once the jump was completed, they received their next clue.

Bungee jumping was first offered in New Zealand as an activity to the public in 1988. The Nevis Bungy Jump, the highest in New Zealand, is not for the faint of heart. From 440 feet above the raging waters of the Nevis River, the free fall lasts 8.4 seconds and has you falling at speeds of more than 80 mph.[19] And the ride to the jump is thrilling as well—the thirty-five-minute journey includes a ride in a four-wheel-drive bus along very steep and windy roads, and then you take a cable car across the gorge to the jumping platform. The minimum age to jump is thirteen years old, and children fourteen and under require adult consent and accompaniment on the jump.[20]

Behind-the-Scenes Snapshot: This was a thrilling jump—my first, and most likely last, bungee jump for the race. I must have stood on the platform for at least five minutes before I had the courage to step off. I remember jumping and trying to scream, but nothing came out; it literally took my breath away. As you reach the end of the free fall, the bungee shoots you back up and you drop again!

How to get there: Fly into Auckland Airport and transfer to a flight to Queenstown Airport. From there rent a car or take a taxi.

☐ Jet Boat Ride at the Shotover River
Season 2, Episode 10, Fast Forward

The Fast Forward required one team to make their way to the Shotover River. There, they had to ride a jet boat and spot a Route Marker flag to find the Fast Forward reward.

World famous for its ultimate jet boat experience, Shotover Jet is the only company allowed to operate in the Shotover River canyons and has thrilled more than 3 million riders since 1970.[21] The unique ride takes you through narrow canyons and can spin you up to 360 degrees. The jet boats are made for speed, traveling up to 56 mph, gliding you over rapids and performing gravity-defying stunts; each ride lasts about twenty-five minutes. Built in Queenstown, the jet boats were designed specifically to handle the Shotover canyons.[22]

> OTHER NEW ZEALAND MUST-SEES!
>
> - MILFORD TRACK
> - LAKE TEKAPO
> - OTAGO CENTRAL RAIL TRAIL
> - HIKING JOSEF AND FOX GLACIERS
> - ABEL TASMAN COAST TRACK

Address: 3 Arthurs Point Road, Central Queenstown, New Zealand

BEHIND THE SCENES

How We Pull It Off

We have an incredible team of talented people working on the show. *The Amazing Race* is an enormous undertaking, and it takes a team of seasoned professionals to pull everything off. The creative and logistics alone take months of planning, and our producers, camera and sound teams, editors, story producers, production designers, challenge producers, researchers, casting team, travel coordinator, visa specialists, accountants, and assistants are all integral parts of the success of our show. We also work with facilitators and their local staff around the world, and after working with us year after year, they have become part of our *Amazing Race* family.

Each season has a very specific timeline. Casting usually takes about four months and while that is happening, the creative for each leg of the race is developed in the preproduction period. This is when we choose the locations and come up with the tasks that will become Detours, Roadblocks, Route Markers, Fast Forwards, and Pit Stops. Bertram and I start with a giant map that spans an entire wall in our office, and using a very low-tech system, we push pins into the map and guide a red string from city to city to map out the route. We are always thinking of new places we would like to go, and places we would love to go back to. Of course, so much more goes into the process (such as budget and logistics), but the map is always our jumping-off point!

Once the locations are selected and research begins, we plan a scouting trip. Bertram and I typically don't scout together; we split up the locations and each travel with a producer, meeting up with a local facilitator to begin our scout. This is not only a logistical puzzle for the show but also a logistical puzzle at home; we have a fourteen-year-old daughter, Ava, and a dog named Lola. Managing schedules can get a bit tricky, to say the least!

Once the contestants have been cast, the route for the season is set, and all locations and challenges have been approved by CBS, we head out to begin the race. Filming usually takes about three and a half weeks, and we shoot every day, rain or shine. Once we begin filming, the footage is sent back to our office so that our editors and story team can begin putting the show together. From preproduction to the final edit, the entire process takes about ten months.

When planning out a race, we have to figure out all the logistics beforehand. This entails researching all possible flights teams could take to their destination, and determining how long it will take them to complete each leg of the race.

This planning goes into a document called "The Fast/Slow." It breaks down the fast, medium, and slow time we estimate a team will need to complete all the tasks in each leg (and we do this for the entire race, from the starting line to the finish line). This is worked out by meticulous testing of the route and challenges months before we start the race.

This is a very useful and planned-out document, but if one team gets lost or has a difficult time completing a task, it will have a domino effect on the entire production. In season 6, teams had to roll out hay bales to find a clue hidden in the center of the hay. All teams had completed the task except for one, who worked at it for over nine hours! Our entire production team was about to miss its flight to the next location, so Phil was taken to the location and had to eliminate the team on the spot. If we had missed the flight, the other teams would have gotten to the next country before us!

One season, the contestants were on a multi-flight jaunt to Italy when our production flight was canceled. We had to get to Italy ahead of the teams, so we booked tickets on a train and made it to the location just in time.

There are so many things that the viewer doesn't get to see while we film the show. During season 5, we were filming on the Giza Plateau at the base of the Great Pyramid in Egypt. We had been outside for hours and our team was getting hungry. Our location manager said he would get us something to eat. About an hour later, a man on horseback arrived carrying several boxes of pizza! It was so unexpected! Pizza delivery on horseback at the base of the Great Pyramid!

Before we leave for the race, there's so much that has to be taken care of *just* to enter a country. We must have valid passports, international customs documents called carnets for every piece of gear and equipment, visas, vaccinations, film permits, flight reservations, and hotel rooms for every person on the staff who travels.

When Phil is at the starting line and says "Go!" there are already hundreds of people on our production team who have advanced to their respective locations. Producers, members of the art department, and members of the challenge department leapfrog ahead while story producers and security and camera teams travel with the contestants.

Our in-country local team consists of a facilitator, location managers, camera crews, an art team, drivers, production assistants, translators, and more. Clues are reviewed, locations prepped, challenges retested, and then once the contestants' flights land, it's time to race!

As teams get eliminated, they're sequestered in a secret location until the last leg of the race. Then we bring them to the finish line so they can cheer on the final three teams as they run to the mat.

The Contestants

Every season, thousands of people send in videos to our casting team. Over the years, we have seen some *very* creative videos of people making up dance routines, singing *Amazing Race*–themed songs, and we have even seen people create mini *Amazing Race* challenges to show us their skills.

Of the thousands of applicants, twenty-five to thirty teams are flown to LA for casting finals. Of that group, we typically cast eleven teams, with two alternate teams. We look for teams that are dynamic and have an interesting story; they're adventurous, competitive, and outspoken.

When filming begins, every team has a camera crew that runs alongside them. The camera crews are fit, fast, and extremely talented, and they run all over the world in all types of weather on all types of terrain to capture the story of each team's personal experience. They run with heavy cameras and sound equipment, taking only a small backpack of personal essentials with them.

There are hundreds of pieces of camera gear and equipment that fly on every flight from location to location; it's astounding to see all the equipment on the baggage claim belt as it comes off the plane. Trolly after trolly is filled with the gear, and vans pick up our team at the airport to take them right to a location to start to set up.

In our earlier seasons, before contestants became savvy in what they brought, we had one team show up at the starting line with Rollerblades! Another season, contestants showed up with full-size luggage with wheels; they got rid of that quickly and used their leg money to buy smaller bags. You will never see a team checking in luggage, as they want to exit the plane and airport as quickly as possible. Most of the production team also travels with small carry-on luggage, as there have been too many times where we have found ourselves with no luggage and no change of clothing! Our time in each country is sometimes so short that by the time the lost luggage arrives, we have already moved on to the next country.

Before filming, our contestants go through several days of orientation, going over rules and safety. Once we start the race, a security team travels with us for the entire trip.

If a moment is missed during filming, we cannot reshoot it; *The Amazing Race* is a competition for $1 million, and in order to be fair, we cannot hold the teams up. Filming the show is like filming a live sporting event: it's continually in motion and keeps moving forward.

There's no stopping the race once we start, but we did once have a close call. In season 1, we were at a desert Pit Stop in Tunisia. In the middle of the night, a huge sandstorm ripped through our campsite and completely destroyed it. We had to evacuate the area and drive the production team and contestants in a caravan of vehicles through the desert to safety.

In the earlier seasons of the *Race*, communication was very difficult; cell phone coverage was extremely limited, and we had to rely on satellite phones to call producers to find out where the teams were. Many times, this did not work, and we would have no idea when contestants would show up to a location. Today, cell phones work just about anywhere in the world, and we have apps like WhatsApp to send information instantly and know exactly where teams are at all times. It literally takes a global village to make this show, and we wouldn't have it any other way.

Countries Visited

North America

- United States (Puerto Rico, Guam & the US Virgin Islands)
- Panama
- Canada
- Mexico
- Costa Rica
- Jamaica
- Trinidad & Tobago

South America

- Brazil
- Argentina
- Chile
- Colombia
- Paraguay
- Peru
- Bolivia
- Ecuador
- Uruguay

Europe

- France
- Germany
- Italy
- Netherlands
- Switzerland
- United Kingdom (England, Northern Ireland, Scotland & Wales)
- Russia

- Austria
- Norway
- Spain
- Sweden
- Poland
- Belgium
- Croatia
- Czech Republic
- Denmark
- Greece
- Iceland
- Portugal

- Ireland
- Turkey
- Estonia
- Finland
- Hungary
- Lithuania
- Liechtenstein
- Malta
- Monaco
- Romania
- Ukraine

Africa

- Morocco
- Tanzania
- South Africa
- Botswana
- Namibia
- Zambia
- Zimbabwe
- Burkina Faso
- Egypt
- Ethiopia

- Ghana
- Kenya
- Madagascar
- Malawi
- Mauritius
- Mozambique
- Senegal
- Seychelles
- Tunisia
- Uganda

Asia

- China (Taiwan, Hong Kong & Macau)
- India
- Japan
- Thailand
- Vietnam
- Indonesia
- Malaysia
- United Arab Emirates
- Cambodia
- the Philippines
- Singapore
- South Korea
- Bangladesh
- Kazakhstan
- Oman
- Sri Lanka
- Armenia
- Azerbaijan
- Bahrain
- Georgia
- Kuwait
- Laos
- Mongolia

Oceania

- Australia
- New Zealand
- French Polynesia

Quick Facts

- Nearly four hundred episodes filmed
- Approximately twenty-three days straight to film a season
- Over 1 million miles traveled in more than twenty years
- More than four hundred flights
- More than seventy-five thousand people have applied to race
- Ninety-three countries visited on six continents
- China is the most visited country: fifteen times
- The U-Turn was introduced in season 12
- In season 14, the first-ever Blind U-Turn was used
- The Express Pass was introduced in season 17; in the last seven seasons, two of the teams that earned the Express Pass have gone on to win *The Amazing Race* (seasons 19 and 20)
- Average number of plane tickets purchased in one season: 1,300
- US edition airs in 130 countries
- Nine international versions of the original show
- Core production team of seventy people
- Two thousand local hires
- Over seven hundred contestants
- Nick and Starr (season 13) were the youngest team to win (at twenty-one and a half years old)
- Doctors and best friends Nat and Kat made *Amazing Race* history in season 17 by becoming the first all-female team to win the race
- Dave and Connor, from season 24, were the first parent-child team to win the race
- Rob and Brennan were the first team to ever win *The Amazing Race*
- Kim and Penn were the oldest couple to win the race
- Jet and Cord, from season 16, were the only team to perform a Speed Bump and come in first in the same leg

- The winners of season 20, Rachel and Dave, won eight legs of the race, setting a new record for most legs won in a single season
- Seasons when the team that wins the first leg has gone on to win the race: 1, 10, 13, 15, 19, 20, 28 (22.5 percent of the time)
- Seasons when a team has won the race after winning only the final leg: 11, 18, 21, 25, 27

Breakdown of Winning Teams

- Fifteen couple teams
- Seven friend teams
- Six sibling teams
- One parent-child team
- One blind date team
- One "strangers" team

Awards

- Ten Primetime Emmys for Best Reality Competition Show
- Three Primetime Emmys for Outstanding Picture Editing for Nonfiction Programming
- Two Primetime Emmys for Outstanding Cinematography for Nonfiction Programming
- Two Producers Guild Awards
- One Directors Guild Award
- One GLAAD Award
- Three Gold Derby Awards
- One Television Critics Award

Thank You!

After more than twenty years and thirty-three seasons, it has certainly been an exciting adventure. We are so grateful to everyone who has ever worked on *The Amazing Race*, taking on the nearly impossible and many times making personal sacrifices. You have missed birthdays, holidays, weddings, anniversaries, and much more, and we thank you and your families; your dedication is truly appreciated.

To our loyal fans, those of you who have watched since season 1 and the new generation that is now seeing the show for the first time, thank you for watching! Thank you for cheering us on year after year! We are excited to see what the future holds and hope to continue making *The Amazing Race*, a show that we are truly passionate about, for many years to come!

ACKNOWLEDGMENTS

First, my biggest thank-you goes to my husband and partner, Bertram van Munster. *The Amazing Race* would not have been possible without you. You live and breathe everything the world has to offer and then some! We've traveled around the world together for nearly twenty-five years, and it has been an incredible adventure. My grandmother told me on our wedding day that I would never be bored; wow, did she know you!

Ava, our amazing daughter, we hope we've inspired you to listen to your heart and find your passion in life.

Thank you, Renée, my wonderful sister, for always being there for our family.

Thank you, CBS, for giving us the opportunity to create something extraordinary that many said could never be done. Producing a groundbreaking show takes a leap of faith, and you stood by us 100 percent.

Thank you, Jerry Bruckheimer, Jonathan Littman, KristieAnne Reed, Phil Keoghan, Mark Vertullo, Darren Bunkley, Pat Cariaga, Matt Schmidt, JR Meyer, Sally Bedding, Micheal DiMaggio, Lynne Spillman, Mary-Pat Carney, Christine Tohme, Dave Feldman, Steve Lafferty, and David Gross, for being instrumental to the success of the show and, most of all, for your friendship.

Thank you to our incredible production crew: camera and sound teams, producers, challenge team, art department, post department, editors, story producers, casting, safety team, accounting, research, and production staff. It takes a small country (not just a village) to make this show a reality.

ACKNOWLEDGMENTS

Thank you to our amazing fans, for watching for more than twenty years! And to our contestants for bringing our ideas to life—sometimes in ways we could never have imagined! Thank you to our facilitators around the world and to all the countries and cities that have welcomed us with open arms.

A big thanks to my editor, Samantha Lubash, who guided me through the process of writing this book.

NOTES

North America

1. "Bethesda Fountain," Central Park, OAD, https://www.centralpark.com/things -to-do/attractions/bethesda-fountain/.

2. "Tour Visitor Centre," United Nations, https://visit.un.org/content/tour.

3. "America's First Pizzeria: Little Italy & Chelsea, NYC," Lombardi's, https://www .firstpizza.com/.

4. "Flushing Meadows Corona Park," Flushing Meadows Corona Park Highlights— Unisphere: NYC Parks, https://www.nycgovparks.org/parks/flushing-meadows -corona-park/highlights/12761.

5. "History," Guardian Building, https://www.guardianbuilding.com/history.

6. Michael Jackman, "How a New Sport Called 'Fowling' Was Born and Brought to Detroit," *Detroit Metro Times*, January 28, 2015, https://www.metrotimes .com/detroit/how-a-new-sport-called-fowling-was-born-and-brought-to-detroit /Content?oid=2295448.

7. "Home of the Original Football Bowling Pin Game," Fowling Warehouse, https:// fowlingwarehouse.com/.

8. "Third Man Records Cass Corridor Detroit," Third Man Records, https:// thirdmanrecords.com/locations/detroit-storefront.

9. Stacy Newman, "Encyclopedia of Detroit," Detroit Historical Society—Where the past is present, https://detroithistorical.org/learn/encyclopedia-of-detroit/fort-wayne.

10. "City Gallery in the Historic Water Tower," City of Chicago, https://www.chicago.gov/city/en/depts/dca/supp_info/city_gallery_in_thehistoricwatertower.html.

11. "Chicago Water Tower," Chicago Architecture Center—CAC, https://www.architecture.org/learn/resources/buildings-of-chicago/building/chicago-water-tower/.

12. "City Gallery in the Historic Water Tower," City of Chicago, https://www.chicago.gov/city/en/depts/dca/supp_info/city_gallery_in_thehistoricwatertower.html.

13. "History Of Deep Dish Pizza—History of Gino's East," Gino's East, https://www.ginoseast.com/history.

14. Ibid.

15. "Wrigley Field History," MLB.com, https://www.mlb.com/cubs/ballpark/information/history.

16. "Wrigley Field Tours," MLB.com, https://www.mlb.com/cubs/ballpark/tours.

17. "Fall in Love with Red Rocks Amphitheatre: Visit Denver," Denver Colorado Vacations & Conventions, https://www.denver.org/things-to-do/music-nightlife/red-rocks/.

18. "Red Rocks Amphitheatre," Red Rocks Amphitheatre, http://www.theredrocksamphitheater.com/.

19. "Hot Air Ballooning: Park City Views & Adventure," https://www.visitparkcity.com/outdoors/hot-air-ballooning/.

20. Ibid.

21. "The Neon Museum Las Vegas: Neon Boneyard," Neon Museum Las Vegas, https://www.neonmuseum.org/the-collection/neon-boneyard.

22. Ibid.

23. "Graceland Chapel—World's First Elvis Wedding Chapel," https://graceland chapel.com/.

24. "Coit Tower," San Francisco Recreation and Parks, CA, https://sfrecpark.org /Facilities/Facility/Details/Coit-Tower-290.

25. Ibid.

26. "History," Golden Gate Fortune Cookie Factory, https://www.goldengatefortune cookies.com/history.

27. Ibid.

28. "Matanuska Glacier," Alaska Guide, https://alaska.guide/Glacier/Matanuska-Glacier.

29. "Travel Alaska—Talkeetna Traveler and Vacation Information," Travel Alaska, https://www.travelalaska.com/Destinations/Communities/Talkeetna.aspx.

30. "Fish Lake Fishing," Hook and Bullet, https://www.hookandbullet.com/fishing -fish-lake-talkeetna-ak/.

31. "Dog Sledding in Alaska: Experience Mushing Like an Iditarod Racer," Alaska .org, https://www.alaska.org/things-to-do/dog-sledding.

32. "Alaska/Practical Information/Transport/Getting Around," *Lonely Planet*, August 8, 2019, https://www.lonelyplanet.com/usa/alaska/narratives/practical-information /transport/getting-around.

33. "Travel Alaska—Getting Around Alaska by Plane," Travel Alaska, https://www .travelalaska.com/Getting-Around/Travel-Within-Alaska/By-Plane.aspx.

34. "Juneau Kayaking Tour & Mendenhall Glacier Viewing," Alaska Shore Excursions, https://alaskashoreexcursions.com/juneau/glacier-view-sea-kayaking-tour.

35. Ibid.

36. "Kalae (South Point) Hawaii Island," Go Hawaii, https://www.gohawaii.com /islands/hawaii-big-island/regions/kau/ka-lae-south-point.

37. "Hawaii Volcanoes National Park, Island of Hawaii," Go Hawaii, January 22, 2020, https://www.gohawaii.com/islands/hawaii-big-island/regions/kau/volcanoes-national-park.

38. Lee Morgan, "Tandem Skydiving in Hawaii," *USA Today*, January 15, 2019, https://traveltips.usatoday.com/tandem-skydiving-hawaii-61704.html.

39. "Kaneohe Bay Sandbar," https://www.hawaiiactivities.com/en/hawaii/oahu/ctg/165886:kaneohe_bay_sandbar/.

40. "History of Stand Up Paddling," SUP, Canoe, Kayak Tours & Maui Surf Lessons, September 9, 2019, https://hawaiianpaddlesports.com/news/history-of-stand-up-paddling/.

41. "8 Best Places to Stand Up Paddle Board in Hawaii," Stand Up Paddle Boarding HeadQuarters, March 27, 2020, https://thesuphq.com/8-best-places-stand-up-paddle-board-sup-in-hawaii/.

42. "Secret Island Beach Activities at Kualoa," Kualoa Ranch, https://www.kualoa.com/toursactivities/secret-island-beach/.

43. "Hawaiian Luau," Go Hawaii, https://www.gohawaii.com/hawaiian-culture/luau.

44. Coco Zickos, "Hawaii Luaus—the Definitive Guide to the Best Luaus in Hawaii," Hawaii.com, December 18, 2020, https://www.hawaii.com/things-to-do/luau/.

45. "Mountain Biking," WinSport, https://www.winsport.ca/explore-winsport/off-season-activities/mountain-biking/.

46. "WinSport's Canada Olympic Park," Family Fun Calgary, https://www.familyfuncanada.com/calgary/canada-olympic-park/.

47. "Sunshine Village," Sunshine Village Ski Resort in Banff Alberta, https://www.skibanff.com/about-destination.

48. "Banff Snowshoeing Tour at Sunshine on Top of the World," White Mountain Adventures, https://www.whitemountainadventures.com/banff-snowshoeing-sunshine-meadows.

49. "Set Sail on the Kajama," Tallship Cruises Toronto, https://www.tallshipcruises toronto.com/.

50. "Astounding—CN Tower," CN Tower, https://www.cntower.ca/en-ca/about-us /history/astounding.html.

51. "Disciplines," Château de Cirque, https://www.chateau-cirque.com/en/disciplines.

52. "Biosphère, Environment Museum," Drapeau, https://www.parcjeandrapeau .com/en/biosphere-environment-museum-montreal/.

53. "Montreal Biosphere," Montreal Biosphere—Montreal, https://imtl.org/montreal /building/biosphere.php.

South America

1. Melissa Locker, "Visit Sugarloaf Mountain," *Travel + Leisure*, August 8, 2016, https://www.travelandleisure.com/trip-ideas/adventure-travel/sugarloaf -mountain-rio.

2. "Abseiling and Rappelling, Outdoor Activities: Rio De Janeiro," *Rio Natural*, https://www.rionatural.com.br/tours/abseiling/.

3. Lorraine Murray, "Christ the Redeemer," *Encyclopedia Britannica*, https://www .britannica.com/topic/Christ-the-Redeemer.

4. Ibid.

5. Sarah Brown, "A Brief History of the Carioca Aqueduct in One Minute," Culture Trip, October 4, 2016, https://theculturetrip.com/south-america/brazil/articles /a-brief-history-of-the-carioca-aqueduct-in-one-minute/.

6. "Escadaria Selarón: A Free Open Air Masterpiece in Rio de Janeiro," Free Walker Tours, https://freewalkertours.com/selaron-staircase/.

7. "Pedra Bonita Mountain: Athletic Paradise," Air France, https://www.airfrance
.com/NZ/en/common/travel-guide/pedra-bonita-mountain-athletic-paradise.htm.

8. "Mercado Municipal Adolfo Lisboa: Manaus, Brazil Attractions," *Lonely Planet*,
https://www.lonelyplanet.com/brazil/the-north/manaus/attractions/mercado
-municipal-adolfo-lisboa/a/poi-sig/1181395/363219.

9. "Mercado Municipal Adolpho Lisboa," *Travel + Leisure*, https://www.travel
andleisure.com/travel-guide/manaus-the-amazon/things-to-do/mercado-municipal
-adolpho-lisboa.

10. "Eva Perón," *Encyclopedia Britannica*, https://www.britannica.com/biography
/Eva-Peron.

11. Kristin Deasy, "Recoleta Cemetery: What to Know About the World's Best
Cemetery," Culture Trip, June 20, 2017, https://theculturetrip.com/south
-america/argentina/articles/recoleta-cemetery-what-to-know-about-the-worlds
-best-cemetery/.

12. "Tango in Buenos Aires," Frommer's, https://www.frommers.com/destinations
/buenos-aires/tango.

13. Celeste Moure, "Campo Argentino De Polo," *Condé Nast Traveler*, https://www
.cntraveler.com/activities/buenos-aires/campo-argentino-de-polo.

14. Sorcha O'Higgins, "The Best Places to Try Chocolate in Bariloche, Argentina,"
Culture Trip, January 19, 2018, https://theculturetrip.com/south-america
/argentina/articles/the-best-places-to-try-chocolate-in-bariloche-argentina/.

15. "Del Turista Chocolates from Bariloche," Patagonia.com.ar, https://www
.patagonia.com.ar/San+Carlos+de+Bariloche/380E_Del+Turista+Chocolates+f
rom+Bariloche.html.

16. "Traditional Asado," Argentina's Travel Guide, http://argentinastravel.com
/basics/cuisine/asado/.

17. "What Is an Asado?" Argentina's Travel Guide, http://argentinastravel.com
/basics/cuisine/asado/what-is-an-asado/.

18. "Fly Atacama Desert," Antofaya Expeditions, http://www.antofaya.com/iqq/.

19. "Zip-Line Cascada de las Animas," Cascada de Las Animas Waterfall of the Spirits, https://www.cascadadelasanimas.cl/en/producto/tirolesa/.

Europe

1. Dylan Thuras, "Paris Sewer Museum," *Atlas Obscura*, https://www.atlasobscura .com/places/paris-sewer-museum.

2. Anna Brooke, "Basilique du Sacré-Coeur," in "Paris—Attraction," Frommer's, https://www.frommers.com/destinations/paris/attractions/basilique-du-sacr -coeur.

3. Ibid.

4. Courtney Traub, "Inside La Coupole, a Montparnasse Brasserie Haunted with Artistic History," Paris Unlocked, https://www.parisunlocked.com/best-of-paris /inside-la-coupole-a-montparnasse-brasserie-haunted-with-artistic-history/.

5. Rick Steves and Steve Smith, "Chamonix Walk," in *Rick Steves' France 2017* (Berkeley, CA: Avalon Travel, 2017).

6. "Chamonix–Mont-Blanc," *Encyclopedia Britannica*, https://www.britannica.com /place/Chamonix-Mont-Blanc.

7. "Best Paragliding in Chamonix," SeeChamonix.com | The Essential Guide to Chamonix, October 28, 2015, https://www.seechamonix.com/paragliding/guide.

8. "Best Watersports to Do in Saint Tropez," SeeSaintTropez, https://www .seesainttropez.com/watersports/guide.

9. "London Eye," *Encyclopedia Britannica*, https://www.britannica.com/place/London -Eye.

10. "About Us," London Eye, https://www.londoneye.com/our-company/about-us/.

11. "Tower Bridge," *Encyclopedia Britannica*, https://www.britannica.com/topic /Tower-Bridge.

12. Ibid.

13. Daniel Gillaspia, "Renting Pedal Boats on the Serpentine in Hyde Park, London," UponArriving: Make Travel Happen, June 10, 2015, https://www.uponarriving .com/renting-pedal-boats-on-the-serpentine-in-hyde-park-london/.

14. Laura Porter, "Camden Market—How to Spend a Day of London Retail Madness," TripSavvy, June 4, 2019, https://www.tripsavvy.com/world-famous -camden-markets-1583506.

15. "Cambridge Punting Lessons," Adventure Connections, https://www.adventure connections.co.uk/ideas/cambridge-punting-lessons/.

16. Priya Khaira-Hanks, "Mail Rail Delivers an Underground History Lesson at London's New Postal Museum," *Guardian*, July 28, 2017, https://www .theguardian.com/travel/2017/jul/28/mail-rail-underground-london-postal -museum.

17. "Blue Lagoon: Iceland Activities," *Lonely Planet*, https://www.lonelyplanet .com/iceland/reykjanes-peninsula/activities/blue-lagoon/a/poi-act/1028801 /1318046.

18. Julie, "20 Best Waterfalls in Iceland & Their Exact Locations," Earth Trekkers, June 10, 2020, https://www.earthtrekkers.com/best-waterfalls-in-iceland/.

19. "Description," Vatnajökull National Park, https://www.vatnajokulsthjodgardur.is /en/areas/melting-glaciers/vatnajokull-ice-cap/description.

20. "Kollensvevet Zipline for Everyone," Kollensvevet, https://www.kollensvevet.no/.

21. "Fagernesfjellet Mountain," GoNorway, http://www.gonorway.no/norway/articles /819.

22. "HotTug Unexpected Freedom—History," de HotTug, https://www.hottug.nl /info_en.htm.

23. "Dutch Cycling Figures," Bicycle Dutch, January 2, 2018, https://bicycledutch .wordpress.com/2018/01/02/dutch-cycling-figures/.

24. Tom Coggins, "7 Must-Visit Markets in the Netherlands," Culture Trip, April 27, 2017, https://theculturetrip.com/europe/the-netherlands/articles/7-must-visit-markets-in-the-netherlands/.

25. "Deutsches Technikmuseum," visitBerlin.de, https://www.visitberlin.de/en/deutsches-technikmuseum.

26. "*Unsere Brauerei Geschichte*: Brauhaus in Berlin Spandau," Brauhaus in Spandau, https://www.brauhaus-spandau.de/brauerei/geschichte/.

27. Pete Dombrosky, "Brauhaus Spandau," Thrillist, https://www.thrillist.com/venue/drink/nation/bar/brauhaus-spandau.

28. "Brandenburg Gate," berlin.de, https://www.berlin.de/en/attractions-and-sights/3560266-3104052-brandenburg-gate.en.html.

29. Ibid.

30. "The Top 11 Places to See What Remains of the Wall," Visit Berlin, February 10, 2020, https://www.visitberlin.de/en/blog/top-11-places-see-what-remains-wall.

31. "East Side Gallery," In Berlin | Visit Berlin, https://www.visitberlin.de/en/east-side-gallery.

32. "Swiss Army Knife," *Encyclopedia Britannica*, https://www.britannica.com/technology/Swiss-Army-knife.

33. "Treille Promenade," Atlas Obscura, https://www.atlasobscura.com/places/treille-promenade.

34. "Gelmer Funicular," Grimselwelt, https://www.grimselwelt.ch/en/transport-lift/gelmer.

35. "Verzasca—007 Golden Eye Bungee Jump," Switzerland Tourism, https://www.myswitzerland.com/en-us/experiences/verzasca-007-golden-eye-bungee-jump/.

36. "Cortina D'Ampezzo Winter Holidays," Dolomiti Superski, https://www.dolomitisuperski.com/en/Experience/Ski-areas/Cortina-d-Ampezzo/Winter-holiday.

37. https://www.inafarawayland.com/cinque-torri-day-hike-dolomites/.

38. Martha Bakerjian, "What to Know About Gondola Rides in Venice," TripSavvy, April 20, 2020, https://www.tripsavvy.com/gondola-rides-in-venice-1548042.

39. Ibid.

40. Ione Wang, "A Guide to the Masks of Venice," Culture Trip, October 23, 2017, https://theculturetrip.com/europe/italy/articles/a-guide-to-the-masks-of -venice/.

41. Ibid.

42. History.com editors, "Pantheon," History.com, https://www.history.com/topics /ancient-greece/pantheon.

43. Ibid.

44. Livia Hengel, "A History of the Altare Della Patria in 60 Seconds," Culture Trip, August 17, 2017, https://theculturetrip.com/europe/italy/articles/a-history-of -the-altare-della-patria-in-60-seconds/.

45. "Piazza Di Spagna & the Spanish Steps: Rome, Italy Attractions," *Lonely Planet*, https://www.lonelyplanet.com/italy/rome/attractions/piazza-di-spagna-the -spanish-steps/a/poi-sig/389877/359975.

46. "Igls Bobsleigh Centre," Tyrol in Austria, https://www.tyrol.com/things-to-do /attractions/all-attractions/a-bobbahn-igls.

47. "Olympiaworld Innsbruck," Olympiaworld Innsbruck, https://www.olympiaworld .at/en/infos-news/olympiaworld-innsbruck/.

48. "VIENNA Now. Forever: Schönbrunn Palace," WienTourismus, https://www .wien.info/en/sightseeing/sights/imperial/schoenbrunn-palace.

49. "VIENNA Now. Forever: Beethoven Museum," WienTourismus, https://www .wien.info/en/music-stage-shows/beethoven-2020/beethoven-museum.

50. "VIENNA Now. Forever: Giant Ferris Wheel," WienTourismus, https://www.wien .info/en/sightseeing/prater/giant-ferris-wheel.

51. "How to Hammam: First Timer's Guide to Turkish Bath," The Guide Istanbul, June 21, 2019, https://www.theguideistanbul.com/first-timers-guide-to-turkish -bath/.

52. "Bath Culture," Ayasofya Hürrem Sultan Hamami, https://www.ayasofyahamami .com/bath_culture.

53. "Grand Bazaar in Istanbul," Go Turkey Tourism, https://www.goturkeytourism .com/things-to-do/grand-covered-bazaar-istanbul-turkey.html.

Africa

1. "Jemaa el-Fnaa," Civitatis Marrakech, https://www.introducingmarrakech.com /jemaa-el-fnaa.

2. "Magic Carpets: The Best Carpet Shopping Spots in Marrakech," Marriott, https://activities.marriott.com/things-to-do/V28Hi37EuZLup7g-magic-carpets -the-best-carpet-shopping-spots-in-marrakech.

3. "What to Expect When Staying in a Moroccan Riad," *On the Go Tours*, August 28, 2018, https://www.onthegotours.com/blog/2018/08/what-to-expect-when -staying-in-a-moroccan-riad/.

4. Ibid.

5. "Deserts of Agafay & Jbilets: How to Select the Best Ride for You," Dunes & Desert, https://www.dunesdeserts.com/en/deserts-of-agafay-jbilets-how-to-select -the-best-ride-for-you/.

6. "The Gharnata Palace," Palais Gharnata—Marrakech, https://www.gharnata .com/en/lepalais.html.

7. Christine Benlafquih, "How to Make Traditional Moroccan Mint Tea," *Spruce Eats*, January 25, 2021, https://www.thespruceeats.com/how-to -make-moroccan-mint-tea-2394995.

8. Amy Tikkanen, "Great Sphinx of Giza," *Encyclopedia Britannica*, https://www .britannica.com/topic/Great-Sphinx.

9. Ibid.

10. Mike Dash, "Inside the Great Pyramid," *Smithsonian*, September 1, 2011, https://www.smithsonianmag.com/travel/inside-the-great-pyramid-75164298/.

11. Ibid.

12. "Giza Camel Rides," Egypt Travel, https://www.google.com/url?q=http://egypt .travel/en/attractions/giza-camel-rides&sa=D&source=editors&ust=16123799 68207000&usg=AOvVaw3P6sSq6pjq0NgydXA9MKVC.

13. "Felucca Sailing," On the Go Tours, January 7, 2020, https://www.onthegotours .com/us/Egypt/Felucca-Sailing.

14. Mark Wiens, "How to Get from Dar es Salaam to Zanzibar," Migrationology, https://migrationology.com/how-to-get-from-dar-es-salaam-to-zanzibar/.

15. "The Doors of Zanzibar," *Preservation Journey*, January 2, 2011, https:// preservationjourney.wordpress.com/2011/01/02/the-doors-of-zanzibar/.

16. Ibid.

17. "Freddie Mercury," *Encyclopedia Britannica*, https://www.britannica.com /biography/Freddie-Mercury.

18. "Freddie Mercury Museum Zanzibar," Freddie Mercury Museum, http:// freddiemercurymuseum.com/.

19. "Darajani Market: Zanzibar Town, Tanzania Attractions," *Lonely Planet*, https://www.lonelyplanet.com/tanzania/zanzibar-archipelago/zanzibar-unguja /attractions/darajani-market/a/poi-sig/1004144/355668.

20. Ibid.

21. Mazuba Kapambwe, "The Best Things to Do at Victoria Falls," The Culture Trip, June 18, 2018, https://theculturetrip.com/africa/zambia/articles/the-best -things-to-see-and-do-at-victoria-falls/.

22. "Victoria Falls Microlight," Victoria Falls Travel Guide, https://www.victoriafalls -guide.net/victoria-falls-microlight.html.

23. "Mosi Oa Tunya," Zambia Tourism, https://www.zambiatourism.com/destinations /national-parks/mosi-oa-tunya/.

24. Ibid.

25. Gary Wockner, "Save the Zambezi—Batoka Gorge Threatened by Huge Dam," International Rafting Federation, https://www.internationalrafting.com/2020/04 /save-the-zambezi-batoka-gorge/.

26. "Horseback Safari in Botswana," African Horse Safaris, https://africanhorse safaris.com/destinations/botswana/.

27. Ibid.

28. "See the Delta by Mokoro," Siyabona Africa, http://www.botswana.co.za /Game_Viewing_Activities-travel/mokoro-experience-dugout-canoe.html.

29. Ibid.

30. "About the Victoria and Alfred Waterfront," V&A Waterfront, https://www .waterfront.co.za/the-va/the-company/about/.

31. Scott Johnson, "A Visit to Robben Island, the Brutal Prison That Held Mandela, Is Haunting and Inspiring," *Smithsonian*, https://www.smithsonianmag.com /travel/robben-island-a-monument-to-courage-62697703/.

32. Ibid.

Middle East

1. "Burj Khalifa," *Encyclopedia Britannica*, https://www.britannica.com/topic/Burj -Khalifa.

2. Peter Graham, "World's Tallest Structure Burj Khalifa Gets a Spy VR Experience," *VRFocus*, February 9, 2018, https://www.vrfocus.com/2018/02/worlds-tallest -structure-burj-khalifa-gets-a-spy-vr-experience/.

3. "Tandem Skydive," Skydive Dubai, https://www.skydivedubai.ae/en/tandem-jumps/requirements.

4. Claudia Capos, "Fast Glimpses of the Past," *Boston Globe*, May 16, 2010, http://archive.boston.com/travel/articles/2010/05/16/fast_glimpses_of_the_past/.

5. "Things to Do in Dubai," Day Out Dubai, https://www.dayoutdubai.ae/blog/things-to-do-in-dubai/.

6. Ibid.

7. Ibid.

8. Megan Honan, "The 10 Best Experiences in Dubai," Culture Trip, May 18, 2020, https://theculturetrip.com/middle-east/united-arab-emirates/articles/best-experiences-in-dubai/.

9. "Now It's Your Turn," Dubai Autodrome, October 6, 2020, https://dubaiautodrome.ae/tracktalk/now-its-your-turn/.

10. "Dubai Gold Souk," Viator, https://www.viator.com/Dubai-attractions/Dubai-Gold-Souk/d828-a1623.

11. "Now It's Your Turn."

12. XDubai, "About," Xline, http://xline.xdubai.com/.

13. Leo, "Leap of Faith in Dubai Is One of the Scariest Waterslides," earthTripper, October 28, 2020, https://earthtripper.com/leap-faith-one-scariest-waterslides-aquaventure-dubai/.

14. "Top Facts About Water Slides & Rides at Atlantis Aquaventure Water Park in Dubai," *Atlantis, the Palm* blog, March 10, 2020, https://blog.atlantisthepalm.com/2020/03/10/top-facts-about-water-slides-rides-at-atlantis-aquaventure-waterpark-in-dubai/.

15. Al Ain Oasis," Visit Abu Dhabi, https://visitabudhabi.ae/en/what-to-see/iconic-landmarks/al-ain-oasis.

16. Ibid.

17. "Wadi Adventure," Visit Abu Dhabi, https://visitabudhabi.ae/en/where-to-go /adventure-and-theme-parks/wadi-adventure.

Asia

1. History.com editors, "Taj Mahal," History.com, June 13, 2011, https://www .history.com/topics/india/taj-mahal.

2. Ibid.

3. Charlotte Dovle, "Mehtab Bagh (Moonlight Garden)—The Best View of Taj Mahal," *Sunshine Seeker*, November 2, 2018, https://www.sunshineseeker .com/destinations/mehtab-bagh-moonlight-garden-best-view-taj-mahal/.

4. "Amber Fort," Incredible India, https://www.incredibleindia.org/content /incredibleindia/en/destinations/jaipur/amber-fort.html.

5. "Amber Fort: India Attractions," *Lonely Planet*, March 29, 2020, https://www .lonelyplanet.com/india/rajasthan/amber/attractions/amber-fort/a/poi-sig /1286368/1329231.

6. "Hawa Mahal: Jaipur, India Attractions," *Lonely Planet*, March 29, 2020, https:// www.lonelyplanet.com/india/rajasthan/jaipur/attractions/hawa-mahal/a/poi -sig/449393/356451.

7. "Fastfacts of Hawa Mahal, the Palace of Breeze," Hawa Mahal, https://www .hawa-mahal.com/fastfacts/.

8. Will Battle, "The Best Street Tea in India: Kolkata's Chai," *Guardian*, February 12, 2017, https://www.theguardian.com/travel/2017/feb/12/kolkata-tea-shacks -chai-daba-foodie.

9. Ibid.

10. Rashmi Gopal Rao, "Mallik Ghat Flower Market," Times of India Travel, June 28, 2016, https://timesofindia.indiatimes.com/travel/Kolkata/Mallik-Ghat-Flower-Market/ps52946781.cms.

11. Ibid.

12. Julie Makinen, "In Beijing, a Wild Ride on Rickshaw," *Los Angeles Times*, October 7, 2012, https://www.latimes.com/world/la-xpm-2012-oct-07-la-fg-china-rickshaws-20121007-story.html.

13. "Great Wall of China," *Encyclopedia Britannica*, https://www.britannica.com/topic/Great-Wall-of-China.

14. Chris Quan, "The Best 10 Sections/Parts of the Great Wall to Visit," China Highlights, February 9, 2021, https://www.chinahighlights.com/greatwall/section/.

15. "Forbidden City," *Encyclopedia Britannica*, https://www.britannica.com/topic/Forbidden-City.

16. Jonathan Chatwin, "Forbidden City at 600: How China's Imperial Palace Survived Against the Odds," CNN, September 18, 2020, https://www.cnn.com/style/article/forbidden-city-china-architecture-600-years/index.html.

17. "Army of Terra-Cotta Warriors: Xi'an, China Attractions," *Lonely Planet*, https://www.lonelyplanet.com/china/shaanxi-shanxi/xian/attractions/army-of-terracotta-warriors/a/poi-sig/1016918/356065.

18. John Roach, "Emperor Qin's Tomb," *National Geographic*, March 23, 2017, https://www.nationalgeographic.com/history/archaeology/emperor-qin/.

19. Harrison Jacobs, "I Tried to Climb the 'Plank Walk' in China Known as 'the Most Dangerous Hike in the World,' but Just Getting There Was the Hardest Part," *Business Insider*, August 19, 2018, https://www.businessinsider.com/china-mount-hua-huashan-most-dangerous-hike-in-the-world-2018-8.

20. "Things to See in Hua Shan," Frommer's, https://www.frommers.com/destinations/hua-shan/attractions/overview.

21. "About HK Tramways," Hong Kong Tramways, https://www.hktramways.com /en/about-hong-kong-tramways/.

22. "Ding-Ding Dreams," *China Daily Hong Kong*, March 18, 2020, https://www .chinadailyhk.com/article/124748.

23. Kate Springer, "Hong Kong's Victoria Peak: Know Before You Go," CNN, https:// www.cnn.com/travel/article/victoria-peak-guide/index.html.

24. "Taekwondo, Experience the Traditional Martial Art of Korea," Imagine Your Korea, https://english.visitkorea.or.kr/enu/ATR/SI_ENG_2_8_7.jsp.

25. Ibid.

26. "Hantan River Rafting: South Korea," Embark.org, https://www.embark.org /south-korea/activity-type/culture/hantan-river-rafting.

27. Mimsie Ladner, "A Guide to South Korea for the Kimchi Obsessed," Culture Trip, April 6, 2018, https://theculturetrip.com/asia/south-korea/articles/a-guide-to -south-korea-for-the-kimchi-obsessed/.

28. Ibid.

29. Geoffrey Morrison, "What It's Like to Stay at a Japanese Capsule Hotel," *Forbes*, July 24, 2016, https://www.forbes.com/sites/geoffreymorrison/2016/07/24 /what-its-like-to-stay-at-a-japanese-capsule-hotel/?sh=477f37381448.

30. "Shibuya Scramble Crossing," Go Tokyo: The Official Tokyo Travel Guide, https:// www.gotokyo.org/en/spot/78/index.html.

31. Joshua Mellin, "Tokyo's Shibuya Crossing: Welcome to the World's Wildest Intersection," CNN, November 14, 2019, https://www.cnn.com/travel/article /shibuya-crossing-tokyo-japan/index.html.

32. Ibid.

33. "Nagano Travel Guide: Access and Things to Do," Japan Rail Pass, November 19, 2020, https://www.jrailpass.com/blog/nagano-travel-guide.

34. "Nagano Olympic Memorial Arena M-WAVE," WAVE, https://www.nagano -mwave.co.jp/m_wave/language/en.php.

35. Caroline Linton, "Revisiting Hanoi, Where John McCain Was Shot Down and Held as a POW," CBS News, August 26, 2018, https://www.cbsnews.com/new /john-mccain-hanoi-hilton-prisoner-of-war-truc-bach-lake/.

36. Ibid.

37. "Halong Bay," *Lonely Planet*, September 8, 2019, https://www.lonelyplanet .com/vietnam/northeast-vietnam/halong-bay.

38. "Halong Bay Full Day Tour with Kayaking or Sampan Boat," Trip.com, https:// www.trip.com/things-to-do/detail/17540717/.

39. Kate O'Malley, "Cruising in Vietnam on the Halong Bay Junk Boats," Vagrants of the World, May 16, 2016, https://vagrantsoftheworld.com /halong-bay-junk-boats-cruising-vietnam/.

40. "Golden Dragon Water Puppet Theater," Tripadvisor, https://www.tripadvisor .com/Attraction_Review-g293925-d1489190-Reviews-Golden_Dragon_Water _Puppet_Theater-Ho_Chi_Minh_City.html.

41. "Reunification Palace," Frommer's, https://www.frommers.com/destinations /ho-chi-minh-city/attractions/reunification-palace.

42. Ibid.

43. "Snow Town Saigon Admission Ticket," Klook Travel, https://www.klook.com /en-US/activity/37813-snow-town-saigon-ticket-ho-chi-minh-city/.

44. "Royal Park Rajapruek," Thailandee.com, https://www.thailandee.com/en/visit -thailand/royal-park-rajapruek-chiang-mai-316.

45. "Royal Park Rajapruek," Chiang Mai Family Guide, November 9, 2019, https:// chiangmaifamilyguide.com/royal-park-rajapruek/.

46. "Everything You Need to Know About Visiting Wat Pho (Temple of the Reclining Buddha)," *U.S. News & World Report*, https://travel.usnews.com/Bangkok _Thailand/Things_To_Do/Temple_of_the_Reclining_Buddha_62500/.

47. "Wat Pho in Bangkok," Hotels.com Go Guides, https://www.hotels.com/go/thailand/wat-pho.

48. "Long Tail Boat Tours," Bangkok River, https://www.bangkokriver.com/place/long-tail-boat-tours/.

49. "Snooker," *Encyclopedia Britannica*, https://www.britannica.com/topic/snooker.

50. "Thailand to Host 2019 World Women's Championship," World Women's Snooker, March 8, 2019, https://www.womenssnooker.com/thailand-to-host-2019-world-womens-championship/.

51. Don Teo, "Enjoy a Meal Among Adorable Cats in Bangkok at Caturday Cat Cafe," Hype & Stuff, September 26, 2019, https://hypeandstuff.com/caturday-cat-cafe-bangkok/.

52. Simone Zeni, "What Is a Century Egg?" *Fine Dining Lovers*, March 15, 2018, https://www.finedininglovers.com/article/what-century-egg.

53. "Jomblang Cave (Goa Jomblang)," Viator, https://www.viator.com/Yogyakarta-attractions/Jomblang-Cave-Goa-Jomblang/d22560-a20736.

54. "Borobudur Temple, Indonesia," Wonderful Indonesia, October 28, 2019, https://www.indonesia.travel/us/en/destinations/java/magelang-regency/borobudur.

55. Ibid.

Oceania

1. "Famously Australian, Uniquely Harry's," Harry's Café de Wheels, https://www.harryscafedewheels.com.au/.

2. "BridgeClimb's Story," BridgeClimb Sydney, https://www.bridgeclimb.com/about-us/bridgeclimb-s-story.

3. "Hyde Park," Sydney.com, https://www.sydney.com/destinations/sydney/sydney -city/city-centre/attractions/hyde-park.

4. "Sydney Opera House," *Encyclopedia Britannica*, https://www.britannica.com /topic/Sydney-Opera-House.

5. "About Us," Sydney Opera House, https://www.sydneyoperahouse.com/general /corporate-information.html.

6. Tom's Working Opal Mine, http://www.tomsworkingopalmine.com/.

7. "Coober Pedy Opal Fields Golf Club," Coober Pedy, https://www.cooberpedy .com/coober-pedy-golf-club/.

8. Scott Eden, "St. Andrews' Kooky Deal with an Australian Golf Club," ESPN, July 10, 2015, https://www.espn.com/golf/story/_/id/13173734/st-andrews-kooky -deal-opal-fields-golf-club.

9. "Auckland Bridge Climb," AJ Hackett Bungy New Zealand, https://www.bungy .co.nz/auckland/auckland-bridge/auckland-bridge-climb/.

10. "Auckland Bridge Climb," Tripadvisor, https://www.tripadvisor.com/Attraction _Review-g255106-d1965840-Reviews-Auckland_Bridge_Climb-Auckland _Central_North_Island.html.

11. "Blokart Sailing," Bay Station at Bay Park, https://www.baystation.co.nz/blokart -sailing/.

12. John Widmer, "A Journey into the Lost World Cave, Waitomo, New Zealand: Review and Tips!" Roaming Around the World, May 20, 2017, https://www .roamingaroundtheworld.com/lost-world-cave-waitomo-new-zealand/.

13. Joe Percival, "Climb Mount Tarawera," AA New Zealand, https://www.aa.co.nz /travel/must-dos-this-summer/climb-mount-tarawera/.

14. Alexandra Diethelm, "Why the Mount Tarawera Crater Walk Is a Must-Do in New Zealand," Discover Aotearoa—New Zealand from N to Z, October 28, 2019, https://www.discover-aotearoa.com/discoveries/mount-tarawera-crater-walk.

15. Brook Sabin, "River Sledging: New Zealand's Craziest Adventure," *Stuff*, November 15, 2019, https://www.stuff.co.nz/travel/experiences/adventure -holidays/117445350/new-zealands-craziest-river-adventure-whitewater -rafting-meets-the-luge.

16. "Sledging Adventure," Raftabout, https://www.raftabout.co.nz/white-water -rafting/sledging-adventure/.

17. "About," Hell's Gate, https://www.hellsgate.co.nz/about.

18. "Experience," Hell's Gate, https://www.hellsgate.co.nz/experience.

19. "Queenstown Nevis Bungy," AJ Hackett Bungy New Zealand, January 31, 2021, https://www.bungy.co.nz/queenstown/nevis/nevis-bungy/.

20. "Bungy—134m Nevis—NZ's Highest Bungy," Everything Queenstown, https:// www.everythingqueenstown.com/bungy-134m-nevis-nzs-highest-bungy-24/.

21. "Shotover Jet," 100% Pure New Zealand, https://www.newzealand.com/us/plan /business/shotover-jet/.

22. "What to Expect During a Jet Boat Ride," Shotover Jet, https://www.shotoverjet. com/experience/shotover-jet-ride/.

INDEX

Note: Italic page numbers refer to illustrations.

A

Abel Tasman Coast Track, New Zealand, 143

Africa
Botswana, 87–88
Egypt, 77–79
map of destinations, *73*
Morocco, 74–77
South Africa, 89–90
Tanzania, 80–82
Zambia, 83–86

Agra, India
Taj Mahal, 102–3
View the Taj Mahal from Mehtab Bagh (Moonlight Garden), 103

Aiguille du Midi, Chamonix, France, 43

Aiguilles Rouges, Chamonix, France, 44

Al Ain, United Arab Emirates
Date Palms at Al Ain Oasis, 99
Ride Down the World's Largest Man-Made River Rapids, 100

Al Ain Oasis Date Palms, Al Ain, United Arab Emirates, 99

Alfred, Prince, 89

Almoravid Koubba, Marrakech, Morocco, 76

Altare della Patria ("the Typewriter"), Rome, Italy, 65–66

Alto Hospicio, Iquique, Chile, 36–37

Amazing Race, The
awards for, 154
contestants of, 148–49
countries visited, 150–52
creation of, xiv–xvi
gratitude for, 155
infrastructure for, xv, 149
logistics of, 145–47
premiere of, xvi
quick facts on, 153–54
scouting trips, 102, 146
timeline of, 145
winning teams, 154

Amber Fort, Jaipur, India, 103–4

Amsterdam, Netherlands
Bicycle around Amsterdam, 54–55
"HotTug" through the City's Canals, 54
Visit the Cheese Market in Alkmarr, 55–56

INDEX

Amwaj Tower Zip-Line, Dubai, United
Arab Emirates, 97
Anchorage, Alaska
Cold Dip in Fish Lake, 14–15
Denali National Park, 15
Ice Climb the Matanuska Glacier, 14
Angel of the Waters (Stebbins), 2
Anne Frank House, Amsterdam,
Netherlands, 56
Arc de Triomphe, Paris, France, 42
Argentina
Buenos Aires, 33–35
San Antonio de Areco, 35–36
arrival tips, xix
Asia
China, 108–13
India, 102–7
Indonesia, 129–30
Japan, 116–18
map of destinations, 101
South Korea, 113–15
Thailand, 124–28
Vietnam, 119–24
Atacama Desert, Iquique, Chile, 36–37
Atlantis Aquaventure Leap of Faith
waterslide, Dubai, United Arab
Emirates, 98
Atlantis Aquaventure Poseidon's
Revenge waterslide, Dubai,
United Arab Emirates, 98–99
ATM bank card, xvii
Attend a Luau, Maui Island, Hawai'i, 20
Auckland, New Zealand, North Island
Climb the Auckland Harbour Bridge,
137–38
Ride in a Blokart, 138
Aussie Football match, Sydney,
Australia, 134

Australia
Coober Pedy, 135–36
Sydney, 132–35
Austria
Innsbruck, 67–68
Vienna, 68–70
Auto Rickshaw at Chandni Chowk
Market, Delhi, India, 105
Autumn Aloft, Park City, Utah, 10
Aya Sofya, Istanbul, Turkey, 71
Ayasofya Hürrem Sultan Hamami,
Istanbul, Turkey, 70–71

B
Badi Palace, Marrakech, Morocco, 76
Banff National Park, Banff, Alberta, 22
Banff Sunshine Village, Banff, Alberta, 22
Bangkok, Thailand
Eat a One-Thousand-Year-Old Egg
from Wat Klang Food Market, 128
other Bangkok must-sees, 128
Play Snooker at a Snooker Club, 127
Take a Long-Tail Boat on Waterways,
126
Temple of the Reclining Buddha
(Wat Pho), 125–26
Bank Safes in Basement of Guardian
Building, Detroit, Michigan, 5
Basilica Cistern, Istanbul, Turkey, 71
Bateaux Mouches, Paris, France, 42
Batoka Gorge, Zimbabwe Border,
Zambia, 86
Beethoven, Ludwig van, 69
Beijing, China
Forbidden City, 109–10
Great Wall of China, 108–9
Ride in a Pedicab, 108
Belgrand, Eugène, 40

Ben Youssef Madrasa, Marrakech, Morocco, 76

Berlin, Germany
Deutsches Technikmuseum, 56–57
Grab a Drink at Brauhaus Spandau, 57
Stand at Site of Berlin Wall, 58–59
Walk through the Brandenburg Gate, 58

Berlin Wall Site, Berlin, Germany, 58–59

Bethesda Fountain and Terrace, New York City, New York, 2

Bhumibol Adulyadej (king of Thailand), 124

Bicycle around Amsterdam, Amsterdam, Netherlands, 54–55

Blokart ride, Auckland, New Zealand, North Island, 138

Blue Lagoon, Grindavik, Iceland, 50

Boating on the Serpentine in Hyde Park, London, United Kingdom, 46–47

Bondi Beach, Sydney, Australia, 134

Borobudur temple, Java, Indonesia, 130

Botswana, Maun (Okavango Delta), 87–88

Brandenburg Gate, Berlin, Germany, 58

Brauhaus Spandau bar, Berlin, Germany, 57

Brazil
Manaus, 32
Rio de Janeiro, 28–31

Brévent Cable Car, Chamonix, France, 43–44

BridgeClimb Sydney, Sydney, Australia, 133

Brooklyn Bridge, New York City, New York, 4

Bruckheimer Television, xv

Buenos Aires, Argentina
Grave of Evita Perón, 33
Indulge in Chocolate at Del Turista Chocolate Factory, 35
Learn to Tango, 34
Watch a Live Polo Match, 34

Bullet Train to Nagano, Tokyo, Japan, 118

Bulsara, Farrokh, 81–82

Bungee Jump off Nevis Highwire Platform, Queenstown, New Zealand, South Island, 142–43

Bungee Jump off Verzasca Dam, Ticino, Switzerland, 62

Burano, Venice, Italy, 64

Burj Khalifa skyscraper, Dubai, United Arab Emirates, 92

Bush Plane, Juneau, Alaska, 15–16

C

Cable Car up Fagernesfjellet Mountain, Narvik, Norway, 53

Cable Car up Mount Hua and Place a Lock on the Railing, Xi'an, China, 111–12

Calgary, Alberta
Hike to the Continental Divide, 22
Mountain Bike at Canada Olympic Park, 21

Cambridge, United Kingdom, Learn How to Punt, 48–49

Camden Market, London, United Kingdom, 47

camera, xviii

Campo Argentino de Polo, Buenos Aires, Argentina, 34

Canada
Calgary, Alberta, 21–22

Canada (*cont.*)
 Hike to the Continental Divide,
  Banff, Alberta, 22
 Montréal, Quebec, 24–25
 Toronto, Ontario, 22–23
Canada Olympic Park, Calgary, Alberta, 21
Canal Cruise, Amsterdam, Netherlands,
  56
Cape Town, South Africa
 Robben Island and Nelson Mandela's
  Prison Cell, 89–90
 Victoria & Alfred Waterfront, 89
Capsule Land Hotel, Tokyo, Japan, 116
Carioca Aqueduct and Walk along
  Escadaria Selarón, Rio de
  Janeiro, Brazil, 30
Carpet Shop at Jemaa el-Fnaa Market,
  Marrakech, Morocco, 74–75
Cascada de las Animas, Santiago, Chile,
  37–38
Cass Corridor neighborhood, Detroit,
  Michigan, 6
Catacombs of Paris, Paris, France, 42
Caturday Cat Café, Bangkok, Thailand,
  127
Ca' Zenobio degli Armeni, Venice, Italy,
  64–65
Chamonix, France
 Paraglide above Chamonix, 43–44
 Place du Triangle de l'Amitié, 43
Champs-Élysées, Paris, France, 42
Chandni Chowk Market, Delhi, India, 105
Changing of the Guard, London, United
  Kingdom, 48
Château de Chantilly, Paris, France, 42
Chatuchak Market, Bangkok, Thailand,
  128
Cheese Market in Alkmaar, Alkmaar,
  Netherlands, 55–56

Chiang Mai, Thailand, Royal Park
  Ratchaphruek, 124–25
Chicago, Illinois
 Chicago Water Tower, 7
 Gino's East Pizza, 8
 Wrigley Field, 8–9
Chicago Cubs, 9
Chicago Water Tower, Chicago, Illinois, 7
Chile
 Iquique, 36–37
 Santiago, 37–38
China
 Beijing, 108–10
 Hong Kong, 112–13
 Xi'an, 110–12
Christ the Redeemer, Rio de Janeiro,
  Brazil, 29
Cinque Torri, Ski Lift to Top of Dolomite
  Mountains, Cortina d'Ampezzo,
  Italy, 62–63
Climb the Auckland Harbour Bridge,
  Auckland, New Zealand, North
  Island, 137–38
Climb the Sydney Harbour Bridge,
  Sydney, Australia, 133
Climb to Top of Sacré-Cœur Basilica,
  Paris, France, 41
clothing
 layers, xviii
 modest dress requirements, xix
clue key
 Detours, xx, xxi
 Fast Forwards, xx
 Final Leg, xxi
 Pit Stops, xx, xxi
 Roadblocks, xx
 Route Markers, xx, xxi
 Speed Bumps, xxi
 U-Turns, xxi

CN Tower, Toronto, Ontario, 23

Coit Tower, San Francisco, California, 12–13

Cold Dip in Fish Lake, Talkeetna, Alaska, 14–15

Colosseum, Rome, Italy, 66

Concert at Red Rocks Amphitheatre, Morrison, Colorado, 9–10

Continental Divide, Calgary, Alberta, 22

Coober Pedy, Australia
Mine for Opal at Tom's Working Opal Mine, 135
Play Golf on the Driest Golf Course in the World, 136

Coober Pedy Opal Fields Golf Club, Coober Pedy, Australia, 136

Copacabana Beach, Rio de Janeiro, Brazil, 31

Corcovado Mountain, Rio de Janeiro, Brazil, 29

Cortina d'Ampezzo, Italy, Take a Ski Lift to the Top of Dolomite Mountains, 62–63

Count the Number of Stairs on the Spanish Steps, Rome, Italy, 66–67

Cross the Shibuya Scramble Intersection, Tokyo, Japan, 117

Cruise in the Toronto Harbor on the *Kajama* Schooner, Toronto, Ontario, 22–23

Cup of Chai in Tea Capital of India, Kolkata, India, 106

currency, converting to local, xvii

customs, respecting of, x

D

Damnoen Saduak Floating Market, Bangkok, Thailand, 128

Darajani Market, Zanzibar, Tanzania, 82

Dar es Salaam ferry, Zanzibar, Tanzania, 80

Date Palms at Al Ain Oasis, Al Ain, United Arab Emirates, 99

Deepu Jewellers, Gold Souk, Dubai, United Arab Emirates, 96

Delhi, India, Ride in an Auto Rickshaw at Chandni Chowk Market, 105

Del Turista Chocolate Factory, San Carlos de Bariloche, Argentina, 35

Denali National Park, Alaska, 15

Denver, Colorado, Concert at Red Rocks Amphitheatre, 9–10

Descend 160 Feet into Jomblang Cave (Goa Jomblang), Yogyakarta, Indonesia, 129

Detours, xx, xxi

Detroit, Michigan
Bank Safes in Basement of Guardian Building, 5
Game of Fowling at Fowling Warehouse, 5–6
Historic Fort Wayne, 6–7
other must-sees, 7
Tour of Third Man Records, 6

Deutsches Technikmuseum, Berlin, Germany, 56–57

Doganieri, Elise
Albuquerque International Balloon Fiesta and, 10–11
at Berlin Wall, 59
Bungee Jump off Nevis Highwire Platform, 142–43
design work of, xiii, xiv
family of, xiii, 2, 9, 59, 78, 146
at Great Wall of China, 109
on historically important locations, 90
idea for travel show, xiv–xv

Doganieri, Elise (*cont.*)
    map of locations, 145
    Nairobi National Park game drive,
      85
    production company of, xv–xvi
    scouting locations, 102, 146
    travel experiences of, xiv
    Victoria Falls microlight flight, 84
Dogsledding in Denali National Park,
    Alaska, 15
Dolomite Mountains Ski Lift, Cortina
    d'Ampezzo, Italy, 62–63
door stopper, xviii
Dubai, United Arab Emirates
    Al Ain Oasis Date Palms, 99
    Atlantis Aquaventure Leap of Faith
      waterslide, 98
    Atlantis Aquaventure Poseidon's
      Revenge waterslide, 98–99
    Burj Khalifa skyscraper, 92
    Dubai Autodrome, 95
    Dubai Frame, 94
    Dubai Garden Glow, 96–97
    Four-by-Four Adventure in Golden
      Dunes of Margham Desert,
      93–94
    Gold Souk, 96
    Margham Dunes, 93
    Ride the World's Longest Urban Zip
      Line, 97
    Ski Dubai, 94–95
    Tandem Skydive over the Desert, 93
    Virtually Jump off the Tallest
      Skyscraper in the World, 92
Dubai Autodrome, Dubai, United Arab
    Emirates, 95
Dubai Desert Conservation Reserve,
    Dubai, United Arab Emirates,
    93–94

Dubai Frame, Dubai, United Arab
    Emirates, 94
Dubai Garden Glow, Dubai, United Arab
    Emirates, 96–97

E

Eastnor Castle, United Kingdom, 48
East Side Gallery (Berlin Wall), Berlin,
    Germany, 58–59
Eat a One-Thousand-Year-Old Egg
    from Wat Klang Food Market,
    Bangkok, Thailand, 128
Edwards, Harry "Tiger," 132
Egypt
    Giza, 77–79
    Luxor, 79
Eiffel Tower, Paris, France, 42
electrical plugs, for international travel,
    xviii
Elsener, Karl, 59–60
emergency contacts, xvii
emergency kit, xviii
England. *See* United Kingdom
Estancia la Porteña de Areco, San Antonio
    de Areco, Argentina, 35–36
Europe
    Austria, 67–70
    France, 40–45
    Germany, 56–59
    Iceland, 50–51
    Italy, 62–67
    map of destinations, *39*
    Netherlands, 54–56
    Norway, 52–53
    Switzerland, 59–62
    Turkey, 70–71
    United Kingdom, 45–49
Explore Largest Buddhist Temple in the
    World, Java, Indonesia, 130

Explore the Okavango Delta in a Makoro (dugout canoe), Maun (Okavango Delta), Botswana, 88

Expo 67, 25

F

Fagernesfjellet Mountain, Narvik, Norway, 53

Fast Forward, xx

Felucca on Nile River, Luxor, Egypt, 79

Ferry from Dar es Salaam to Zanzibar, Zanzibar, Tanzania, 80

Final Leg, xxi

Fish Lake, Talkeetna, Alaska, 14–15

Flushing Meadows–Corona Park, Queens, New York, 4

Fly in a Bush Plane, Juneau, Alaska, 15–16

Fly in a Microlight Plane over Victoria Falls, Victoria Falls, Zambia, 83–84

Fly on the Trapeze at Le Château de Cirque, Montréal, Quebec, 24

Fondazione Querini Stampalia, gondola from, Venice, Italy, 63–64

Forbidden City, Beijing, China, 109–10

Four-by-Four Adventure in Golden Dunes of Margham Desert, Dubai, United Arab Emirates, 93–94

Fowling Warehouse, Hamtramck, Michigan, 5–6

France
Chamonix, 43–44
Paris, 40–42
Saint-Tropez, 44–45

Frank, Anne, 56

Freddie Mercury's childhood home, Zanzibar, Tanzania, 81–82

Fuller, Buckminster, 25

Funicular Railway Ascensor Artilleria, Santiago, Chile, 38

G

Galata Tower, Istanbul, Turkey, 71

Gallerie Dell'Accademia, Venice, Italy, 64

Game Drive at Mosi-Oa-Tunya National Park, Victoria Falls, Zambia, 84–85

Game of Fowling at Fowling Warehouse, Hamtramck, Michigan, 5–6

Gaucho experience, San Antonio de Areco, Argentina, 35–36

Gaudí, Antoni, 60

Gelmerbahn funicular, Grimsel Pass, Switzerland, 61

Geneva, Switzerland
Promenade de la Treille, 60
Victorinox Swiss Army Knife customization, 59–60

Germany, Berlin, 56–59

Get Your Picture Taken at Victoria Peak, Hong Kong, China, 113

Giant Swing, Bangkok, Thailand, 128

Giethoorn, Netherlands, 56

Gino's East Pizza, Chicago, Illinois, 8

Giza, Egypt
Great Pyramid, 78–79
Sphinx, 77

Goat's Eye Mountain, Banff, Alberta, 22

Golden Dragon Water Puppet Theater Show, Ho Chi Minh City, Vietnam, 122

Golden Dunes of Margham Desert with Four-by-Four, Dubai, United Arab Emirates, 93–94

GoldenEye (film), 62

Golden Gate Fortune Cookie Factory, San Francisco, California, 13

Gold Souk, Dubai, United Arab Emirates, 96

Gondola Ride, Venice, Italy, 63–64

Gorbachev, Mikhail, 58

Go River Sledging on the Kaituna River, Rotorua District, New Zealand, North Island, 140

Go Spelunking at the Waitomo Caves, Waitomo District, New Zealand, North Island, 138–39

Go to the Top of CN Tower, Toronto, Ontario, 23

Go to the Top of Hawa Mahal (Palace of the Winds), Jaipur, India, 104

Go White-Water Rafting down the Hantan River, Seoul, South Korea, 114

Graceland Wedding Chapel, Las Vegas, Nevada, 12

Grand Canal, Venice, Italy, 64

Grand Palace, Bangkok, Thailand, 128

Grave of Evita Perón, Buenos Aires, Argentina, 33

Great American Music Hall, San Francisco, California, 13

Great Chicago Fire of 1871, 7

Great Pyramid, Giza, Egypt, 78–79

Great Wall of China, Beijing, China, 108–9

Grimsel Pass, Switzerland, Ride the Gelmerbahn Funicular, 61

Guardian Building, Detroit, Michigan, 5

H

Hachiko statue (Akita dog), Tokyo, Japan, 117

Hale'mau'mau Crater, Hawai'i Volcanoes National Park, Hawai'i Island, Hawai'i, 18

Ha Long Bay, Vietnam

Take a Cruise on a Junk, 121

Take a Local Boat Called a Sampan, 120–21

Hamptons, Long Island, 2, 4

Hang Glide from the Top of Pedra Bonita Mountain, Rio de Janeiro, Brazil, 31

Hanoi, Vietnam

Hoa Lò Prison, 119–20

Prepare Vietnam's National Dish, Pho, in a Cooking Class, 120

Hantan River, Seoul, South Korea, 114

Harbor Cruise from Circular Quay, Sydney, Australia, 134

Harry, Prince, 132

Harry's Café de Wheels, Sydney, Australia, 132

Hart Plaza, Detroit, Michigan, 7

Haussmann, Georges Eugène, baron, 40

Hawai'i Island, Hawai'i

Hike Hawai'i Volcanoes National Park, 18

Ka Lae, 17

Hawai'i Volcanoes National Park, Hawai'i Island, Hawai'i, 18

Hawa Mahal (Palace of the Winds), Jaipur, India, 104

Heidelberg Project, Detroit, Michigan, 7

Heiligenstadt Testament Site (Beethoven), Vienna, Austria, 69

Helicopter Ride at Night, Las Vegas, Nevada, 12

Helicopter Tour over Rio de Janeiro, Brazil, 29–30

Hemingway, Ernest, 42

Henry VIII (king of England), 47

Hepburn, Audrey, 66

Hi-End Snooker Club, Bangkok, Thailand, 127

Hike Hawai'i Volcanoes National Park, Hawai'i Island, Hawai'i, 18

Hike to the Continental Divide, Calgary, Alberta, 22

Hiking Josef and Fox Glaciers, New Zealand, 143

Historic Fort Wayne, Detroit, Michigan, 6–7

Hoa Lò Prison museum, Hanoi, Vietnam, 119

Ho Chi Minh City, Vietnam
    Golden Dragon Water Puppet Theater Show, 122
    Reunification Palace, 123
    Skiing and Sledding Indoors at Snow Town Saigon, 123–24

Holmenkollen Ski Jump, Oslo, Norway, 52–53

Hong Kong, China
    Get Your Picture Taken at Victoria Peak, 113
    Ride the Hong Kong Tramway ("Ding Ding"), 112

Horseback Safari, Maun (Okavango Delta), Botswana, 87

Hot-Air Balloon Ride, Park City, Utah, 10–11

HotTug through the City's Canals, Amsterdam, Netherlands, 54

Hyde Park, London, United Kingdom, 46–47

Hyde Park, Sydney, Australia, 133–34

I

Ice Climb the Matanuska Glacier, Anchorage, Alaska, 14

Iceland, Reykjavík, 50–51

India
    Agra, 102–3
    Delhi, 105
    Jaipur, 103–4
    Kolkata, 106–7

Indian tea tasting ceremony, Kolkata, India, 106

Indonesia
    Java, 130
    Yogyakarta, 129

Innsbruck, Austria, Olympic Bobsled Track and Ice Rink, 67–68

Ipanema Beach, Rio de Janeiro, Brazil, 31

Iquique, Chile, Paraglide from Alto Hospicio to the Beach, 36–37

Istanbul, Turkey
    Experience a Traditional Turkish Bath, 70–71
    Kapaliçarşi (Grand Bazaar), 71
    other Istanbul must-sees, 71

Italy
    Cortina d'Ampezzo, 62–63
    Rome, 65–67
    Venice, 63–65

J

Jaipur, India
    Amber Fort, 103–4
    Go to the Top of Hawa Mahal (Palace of the Winds), 104

Japan
    Nagano, 118
    Tokyo, 116–18

Japan Rail Pass, 118

Jardim Botânico (Botanical Garden), Rio de Janeiro, Brazil, 31

Java, Indonesia, Explore Largest Buddhist Temple in the World, 130

Jemaa el-Fnaa Market, Marrakech, Morocco, 74–75
Jet Boat Ride at Shotover River, Queenstown, New Zealand, South Island, 143
John, Elton, 132
Jomblang Cave (Goa Jomblang), Yogyakarta, Indonesia, 129
Josef and Fox Glaciers, New Zealand, 143
Jump by Rope Swing into Batoka Gorge, Zimbabwe Border, Zambia, 86
Juneau, Alaska
    Fly in a Bush Plane, 15–16
    Sea Kayaking in the Taku Inlet, 16
junk boat cruise, Ha Long Bay, Vietnam, 121

K

Kaituna River, Rotorua District, New Zealand, North Island, 140
Ka Lae, Southernmost Point in the US, Hawai'i Island, Hawai'i, 17
Kaneohe Bay, Oahu Island, Hawai'i, 18–19
Kapalıçarşı (Grand Bazaar), Istanbul, Turkey, 71
Kaulana Bay, Hawai'i Island, Hawai'i, 17
Kenya, hot-air balloon safari in, 11
Keoghan, Phil
    on *Amazing Race*, xi–xii, 2
    in Amsterdam, 55
    early travel experiences of, ix, x–xi
    Final Leg and, xxi
Keukenhof Gardens, Lisse, Netherlands, 56
Khafre (pharaoh of Egypt), 77
Khufu (pharaoh of Egypt), 78

Kilauea, Hawai'i Volcanoes National Park, Hawai'i Island, Hawai'i, 18
Kiz Kulesi (Maiden's Tower), Istanbul, Turkey, 71
Knife Edge Bridge at Victoria Falls, Victoria Falls, Zambia, 83–84
Kolkata, India
    Cup of Chai in Tea Capital of India, 106
    Mallik Ghat Flower Market, 107
Kolkata Town Hall, Kolkata, India, 106
Koutoubia Mosque, Marrakech, Morocco, 76

L

La Coupole Brasserie, Paris, France, 42
Lake Tekapo, New Zealand, 143
Las Vegas, Nevada
    Graceland Wedding Chapel, 12
    Neon Museum's "Boneyard," 11
    other must-sees, 12
Las Vegas Motor Speedway, Las Vegas, Nevada, 12
Las Vegas Strip, Las Vegas, Nevada, 12
La Treille Park, Geneva, Switzerland, 60
Leap of Faith waterslide, Dubai, United Arab Emirates, 98
Learn How to Make Kimchi, Seoul, South Korea, 115
Learn How to Punt, Cambridge, United Kingdom, 48–49
Le Château de Cirque (Trapezium), Montréal, Quebec, 24
Littman, Jonathan, xv
Live Like a Gaucho, San Antonio de Areco, Argentina, 35–36
local people, meeting of, xi

INDEX

Lombardi's Pizza, New York City, New York, 3

London, United Kingdom

Boating on the Serpentine in Hyde Park, 46–47

Camden Market, 47

Changing of the Guard, 48

Ride the London Eye, 45–46

Ride the Underground Mail Rail, 49

Somerset House, 48

Tower Bridge, 46

Victoria Tower Gardens, 48

London Eye (cantilevered observation wheel), London, United Kingdom, 45–46

Longest Wooden Bench, Geneva, Switzerland, 60

Long-Tail Boat on Waterways, Bangkok, Thailand, 126

Lookout Mountain, Banff, Alberta, 22

Louvre Museum, Paris, France, 42

Luau, Maui Island, Hawai'i, 20

luggage, xviii, 148–49

Luna Park, Sydney, Australia, 134

Luxor, Egypt, Take a Felucca on the Nile, 79

M

McCain, John, 119

Magere Brug (Skinny Bridge), Amsterdam, Netherlands, 56

Mail Rail, London, United Kingdom, 49

makoro (dugout canoe), Maun (Okavango Delta), Botswana, 88

Mallik Ghat Flower Market, Kolkata, India, 107

Manara Gardens, Marrakech, Morocco, 76

Manaus, Brazil, Mercado Municipal Adolpho Lisboa, 32

Mandela, Nelson, 89–90

Margham Dunes, Dubai, United Arab Emirates, 93–94

Marrakech, Morocco

Carpet Shop at Jemaa el-Fnaa Market, 74–75

other Marrakech must-sees, 76

Palais Gharnata, 76–77

Ride Quad Bikes through the Desert, 75–76

Stay in a Riad, 75

Matanuska Glacier, Anchorage, Alaska, 14

Maui Island, Hawai'i, Luau, 20

Maun (Okavango Delta), Botswana

Explore the Okavango Delta in a Makoro (dugout canoe), 88

Horseback Safari, 87

Mauno Loa, Hawai'i Volcanoes National Park, Hawai'i Island, Hawai'i, 18

medical history, xvii

medications

list of, xvii

packing extra medications, xviii

Mehtab Bagh (Moonlight Garden), Agra, India, 103

Mendenhall Glacier, Juneau, Alaska, 16

Mercado Municipal Adolpho Lisboa, Manaus, Brazil, 32

Mercury, Freddie (Farrokh Bulsara), 81–82

Middle East

map of destinations, 91

United Arab Emirates, 92–100

Milford Track, New Zealand, 143

Mine for Opal at Tom's Working Opal Mine, Coober Pedy, Australia, 135

Ming Dynasty, 109

Mirja Raja Singh, 104

Misir Carsisi (Spice Bazaar), Istanbul, Turkey, 71

Mont Blanc, Chamonix, France, 43

Montréal, Quebec
Fly on the Trapeze at Le Château de Cirque, 24
Montréal Biosphère Museum, 25

Monumento Nazionale a Vittorio Emanuele II (National Monument to Victor Emmanuel II), Rome, Italy, 65–66

Moroccan mint tea, Palais Gharnata, Marrakech, Morocco, 76–77

Morocco, Marrakech, 74–77

Mosi-Oa-Tunya National Park Game Drive, Victoria Falls, Zambia, 84–85

Motown Museum, Detroit, Michigan, 7

Moulin Rouge, Paris, France, 42

Mountain Bike at Canada Olympic Park, Calgary, Alberta, 21

Mount Hua, Xi'an, China, 111–12

Mount Standish, Banff, Alberta, 22

Mount Tarawera, Rotorua District, New Zealand, North Island, 139–40

Mouth of Truth (Bocca della Verita), Rome, Italy, 66

Mozart, Wolfgang Amadeus, 68

Mugyewon Arts & Cultural Center, Seoul, South Korea, 115

Murano, Venice, Italy, 64

Museum of Qin Terra-Cotta Warriors and Horses, Xi'an, China, 110–11

M-Wave Olympic Arena, Nagano, Japan, 118

N

Nagano, Japan, Take a Bullet Train to Nagano and Skate on the Olympic Track, 118

Narvik, Norway, Ride the Cable Car up Fagernesfjellet Mountain, 53

Neon Museum's "Boneyard," Las Vegas, Nevada, 11

Neruda, Pablo, 38

Netherlands
Amsterdam, 54–56
other Netherlands must-sees, 56

Nevis Highwire Platform, Queenstown, New Zealand, South Island, 142–43

New York City, New York
Bethesda Fountain and Terrace, 2
Lombardi's Pizza, 3
other New York must-sees, 4
Unisphere, 4
United Nations Headquarters, 3

New York World's Fair of 1964–65, 4

New Zealand, North Island
Auckland, 137–38
other New Zealand must-sees, 143
Rotorua District, 139–41
Waitomo District, 138–39

New Zealand, South Island
other New Zealand must-sees, 143
Queenstown, 142–43

Ngo Dinh Diem, 123

Nile River, Luxor, Egypt, 79

noise-canceling headphones, xviii

North America
Canada, 21–25

map of destinations, *1*
United States, 2–20
Norway
   Narvik, 53
   Oslo, 52–53
Notre-Dame Cathedral, Paris, France, 42

O

Oahu Island, Hawai'i
   Skydive over Oahu, 18–19
   Stand-Up Paddle Boarding at Secret
      Island, Kualoa Ranch, 19–20
Obelisco Sallustiano, Rome, Italy, 66
Oceania
   Australia, 132–36
   map of destinations, *131*
   New Zealand, North Island, 137–41
   New Zealand, South Island, 142–43
Okavango Delta (Maun), Botswana,
   87–88
Olympiahalle, Innsbruck, Austria, 67–68
Olympiaworld, Innsbruck, Austria, 67–68
Olympic Bobsled Track and Ice Rink,
   Innsbruck, Austria, 67–68
Opal Quest Mine, Tom's Working Opal
   Mine, Coober Pedy, Australia, 135
Oracle Park, San Francisco, California, 13
Oslo, Norway, Zip-Line down
   Holmenkollen Ski Jump, 52–53
Otago Central Rail Trail, New Zealand,
   143

P

Pablo Neruda's Home, La Sebastiana,
   Santiago, Chile, 38
packing tips, xviii
Palacio Baburizza, Santiago, Chile, 38
Palais Gharnata, Marrakech, Morocco,
   76–77

Pampelonne Beach, Saint-Tropez,
   France, 44–45
Pantheon, Rome, Italy, 65–66
Paraglide above Chamonix, Chamonix,
   France, 43–44
Paraglide from Alto Hospicio to the
   Beach, Iquique, Chile, 36–37
Paris, France
   Climb to Top of Sacré-Cœur Basilica,
      41
   other Paris must-sees, 42
   Royal Platter at La Coupole
      Brasserie, 42
   Walk the Underground Sewers,
      40–41
Paris Sewer Museum (Musée des
   Égouts de Paris), 40
Park City, Utah, Hot-Air Balloon Ride,
   10–11
passports, xvii
Patscherkofel, Innsbruck, Austria,
   67–68
Peck, Gregory, 66
pedicab, Beijing, China, 108
Pedra Bonita Mountain, Rio de Janeiro,
   Brazil, 31
Perón, Evita, 33
Perón, Juan, 33
Pho Cooking Class, Hanoi, Vietnam,
   120
Piazza del Popolo, Rome, Italy, 66
Piazza Navona, Rome, Italy, 66
Picasso, Pablo, 42
Pit Stop, xxii, xxiii
Place du Triangle de l'Amitié (Triangle of
   Friendship), Chamonix, France,
   43–44
planning, extending journey with, ix
Playa Brava, Iquique, Chile, 36–37

Playa Huayquique, Iquique, Chile, 36–37
Play Golf on the Driest Golf Course
in the World, Coober Pedy,
Australia, 136
Play Snooker at a Snooker Club,
Bangkok, Thailand, 127
Polo Match, Buenos Aires, Argentina,
34
Pont Alexandre III, Paris, France, 42
Ponte delle Guglie, gondola from,
Venice, Italy, 63–64
Ponte Sant'Angelo, Rome, Italy, 66
portable chargers, xviii
Poseidon's Revenge waterslide, Dubai,
United Arab Emirates, 98–99
Postal Museum, London, United
Kingdom, 49
Post Office Railway (Mail Rail), London,
United Kingdom, 49
Prepare Vietnam's National Dish, Pho,
in a Cooking Class, Hanoi,
Vietnam, 120
Presley, Elvis, impersonators of, 12
Promenade de la Treille, Geneva,
Switzerland, 60
Punting, Cambridge, United Kingdom,
48–49

Q
Queenstown, New Zealand, South Island
Bungee Jump off Nevis Highwire
Platform, 142–43
Jet Boat Ride at Shotover River, 143

R
Reagan, Ronald, 58
Redmond, Alice Mae, 8
Red Rocks Amphitheatre, Morrison,
Colorado, 9–10

Reunification Palace, Ho Chi Minh City,
Vietnam, 123
Reykjavík, Iceland
Ride Snowmobiles on a Glacier, 51
Seljalandsfoss Waterfall, 50–51
Swim in the Blue Lagoon, 50
Riads (Moroccan houses), Marrakech,
Morocco, 75
Rialto Bridge, Venice, Italy, 64
Ride Down the World's Largest Man-
Made River Rapids, Al Ain,
United Arab Emirates, 100
Ride in a Blokart, Auckland, New
Zealand, North Island, 138
Ride in an Auto Rickshaw at Chandni
Chowk Market, Delhi, India, 105
Ride in a Pedicab, Beijing, China, 108
Ride Quad Bikes through Desert,
Marrakech, Morocco, 75–76
Ride the Hong Kong Tramway ("Ding
Ding"), Hong Kong, China, 112
Ride the World's Longest Urban Zip Line,
Dubai, United Arab Emirates, 97
Rijksmuseum, Amsterdam, Netherlands,
56
Rio de Janeiro, Brazil
Carioca Aqueduct and Walk along
Escadaria Selarón, 30
Christ the Redeemer, 29
Go to the Top of Sugarloaf Mountain,
28
Hang Glide from the Top of Pedra
Bonita Mountain, 31
Helicopter Tour over, 29–30
other Rio must-sees, 31
Roadblocks, xx
Robben Island and Nelson Mandela's
Prison Cell, Cape Town, South
Africa, 89–90

Roman Forum, Rome, Italy, 66
Roman Holiday (film), 66
Rome, Italy
 Count the Number of Stairs on the
  Spanish Steps, 66–67
 other Rome must-sees, 66
 Pantheon and the Altare della Patria
  ("the Typewriter"), 65–66
Rookwood pottery, 5
Rotorua District, New Zealand, North
 Island
 Go River Sledging on the Kaituna
  River, 140
 Run down the Mouth of a Dormant
  Volcano, 139–40
 Tikitere (Hell's Gate) geothermal
  mud bath, 141
Route Markers, xx, xxi
Royal Botanical Gardens, Sydney,
 Australia, 134
Royal Palace Amsterdam, Amsterdam,
 Netherlands, 56
Royal Park Ratchaphruek, Chiang Mai,
 Thailand, 124–25
Royal Platter at La Coupole Brasserie,
 Paris, France, 42
Rumeli Hisari, Istanbul, Turkey, 71
Run across Knife Edge at Victoria Falls,
 Victoria Falls, Zambia, 83–84
Run down the Mouth of a Dormant
 Volcano, Rotorua District, New
 Zealand, North Island, 139–40

S
Saadian Tombs, Marrakech, Morocco,
 76
Sacré-Cœur Basilica, Paris, France, 41
Sailing Lessons, Saint-Tropez, France,
 44–45

St. Mark's Basilica, Venice, Italy, 64
St. Mark's Square, Venice, Italy, 64
Saint-Tropez, France, Sailing Lessons,
 44–45
Salt Flats, Las Vegas, Nevada, 12
sampan boat, Ha Long Bay, Vietnam,
 120–21
San Antonio de Areco, Argentina, Live
 Like a Gaucho, 35–36
San Francisco, California
 Coit Tower, 12–13
 Golden Gate Fortune Cookie Factory,
  13
 other San Francisco must-sees, 13
Santiago, Chile
 other Santiago must-sees, 38
 Zip Line at Cascada de las Ánimas,
  37–38
Sawai Pratap Singh (Maharaja), 104
Schönbrunn Palace, Vienna, Austria,
 68–69
Sea Kayaking in the Taku Inlet, Juneau,
 Alaska, 16
Secret Island, Kualoa Ranch, Oahu
 Island, Hawai'i, 19–20
Selarón, Jorge, 30
Selarón Steps (Escadaria Selarón), Rio
 de Janeiro, Brazil, 20
Seljalandsfoss waterfall, Reykjavík,
 Iceland, 50–51
Seoul, South Korea
 Go White-Water Rafting down the
  Hantan River, 114
 Learn How to Make Kimchi, 115
 Taekwondo Class, 113–14
Seoul Kimchi Academy, 115
Serpentine in Hyde Park, London,
 United Kingdom, 46–47
Shah Jahan (emperor of India), 102, 103

Shaw, George Bernard, 141

Shibuya Scramble Intersection Crossing, Tokyo, Japan, 117

Shotover River, Queenstown, New Zealand, South Island, 143

Sinatra, Frank, 132

Ski Dubai, Dubai, United Arab Emirates, 94–95

Skiing and Sledding Indoors at Snow Town Saigon, Ho Chi Minh City, Vietnam, 123–24

Ski Museum, Oslo, Norway, 52

Skydive over Oahu, Oahu Island, Hawai'i, 18–19

Snowmobiles on a Glacier, Vatnajökull National Park, Gardabaer, Iceland, 51

Snow Town Saigon, Ho Chi Minh City, Vietnam, 123–24

SolarShuttle of Hyde Park, London, United Kingdom, 47

Somerset House, London, United Kingdom, 48

South Africa, Cape Town, 89–90

South America
  Argentina, 33–36
  Brazil, 28–32
  Chile, 36–38
  map of destinations, 27

South Korea, Seoul, 113–15

Spanish Steps, Rome, Italy, 66–67

Speed Bump, xxi

Sphinx, Giza, Egypt, 77

Stand-Up Paddle Boarding at Secret Island, Kualoa Ranch, Oahu Island, Hawai'i, 19–20

Statue of Liberty, New York City, New York, 4

Stay in a Capsule Hotel, Tokyo, Japan, 116

Stebbins, Emma, 2

Stonehenge, Amesbury, United Kingdom, 48

Stone Town and Royal Doors, Zanzibar, Tanzania, 81

Sugarloaf Mountain, Rio de Janeiro, Brazil, 28

Sunset Point, Detroit, Michigan, 7

Swiss Army Knife customization, Geneva, Switzerland, 59–60

Switzerland
  Geneva, 59–60
  Grimsel Pass, 61
  Ticino, 62

Sydney, Australia
  Climb the Sydney Harbour Bridge, 133
  Harry's Café de Wheels, 132
  other Sydney must-sees, 134
  Sydney Opera House, 134–35
  Walk through Hyde Park, 133–34

Sydney Harbour Bridge, Sydney, Australia, 133

Sydney Opera House, Sydney, Australia, 134–35

Sydney Tower, Sydney, Australia, 134

T

Taekwondo Class, Seoul, South Korea, 113–14

Taj Mahal, Agra, India, 102–3

Take a Bullet Train to Nagano and Skate on the Olympic Track, Nagano, Japan, 118

Take a Cable Car up Mount Hua and Place a Lock on the Railing, Xi'an, China, 111–12

Take a Cruise on a Junk, Ha Long Bay, Vietnam, 121

Take a Ferry from Dar es Salaam to Zanzibar, Zanzibar, Tanzania, 80

Take a Local Boat Called a Sampan, Ha Long Bay, Vietnam, 120–21

Take a Long-Tail Boat on Waterways, Bangkok, Thailand, 126

Taku Glacier, Juneau, Alaska, 16

Taku Inlet, Juneau, Alaska, 16

Tandem Skydive over the Desert, Dubai, United Arab Emirates, 93

Tango Lessons, Buenos Aires, Argentina, 34

Tanneries, Marrakech, Morocco, 76

Tanzania, Zanzibar, 80–82

Teatro Municipal, Rio de Janeiro, Brazil, 31

Temple of the Reclining Buddha (Wat Pho), Bangkok, Thailand, 125–26

Thailand
    Bangkok, 125–28
    Chiang Mai, 124–25

Thamalakane River, Maun (Okavango Delta), Botswana, 88

Third Man Records, Detroit, Michigan, 6

Ticino, Switzerland, Bungee Jump off Verzasca Dam, 62

Tikitere (Hell's Gate) geothermal mud bath, Rotorua District, New Zealand, North Island, 141

Times Square, New York City, New York, 4

Tokyo, Japan
    Bullet Train to Nagano, 118
    Cross the Shibuya Scramble Intersection, 117
    Stay in a Capsule Hotel, 116

Tonga Room at Fairmont Hotel, San Francisco, California, 13

Topkapi Palace, Istanbul, Turkey, 71

Toronto, Ontario
    Cruise in the Toronto Harbor on the *Kajama* Schooner, 22–23
    Go to the Top of CN Tower, 23

Tour of Golden Gate Fortune Cookie Factory, San Francisco, California, 13

Tour of Schönbrunn Palace, Vienna, Austria, 68–69

Tour of Third Man Records, Detroit, Michigan, 6

Tour of USS *Hornet*, San Francisco, California, 13

Tower Bridge, London, United Kingdom, 46

Trapezium (Le Château de Cirque), Montréal, Quebec, 24

travel checklist
    arrival tips, xix
    packing tips, xviii
    prior to departure, xvii–xviii

traveling alone, xviii

Trevi Fountain, Rome, Italy, 66

Turkey, Istanbul, 70–71

Turkish bath, Istanbul, Turkey, 70–71

Tutankhamun (pharaoh of Egypt), 78

U

Underground Mail Rail, London, United Kingdom, 49

Underground Sewers, Paris, France, 40–41

Unisphere, New York City, New York, 4

United Arab Emirates
    Al Ain, 99–100
    Dubai, 92–99

United Kingdom
    Cambridge, 48–49
    Eastnor Castle, 48

United Kingdom (*cont.*)
    London, 45–48
    other United Kingdom must-sees, 48
    Stonehenge, Amesbury, 48
United Nations Headquarters, New York City, New York, 3
United States
    Anchorage, Alaska, 14–15
    Chicago, Illinois, 7–9
    Denver, Colorado, 9–10
    Detroit, Michigan, 5–7
    Hawai'i Island, Hawai'i, 17–18
    Juneau, Alaska, 15–16
    Las Vegas, Nevada, 11–12
    Maui Island, Hawai'i, 20
    New York City, New York, 2–4
    Oahu Island, Hawai'i, 18–20
    Park City, Utah, 10–11
    San Francisco, California, 12–13
Uskudar Ferry, Istanbul, Turkey, 71
USS *Hornet* Tour, San Francisco, California, 13
U-Turn, xxi

V
vaccinations, xvii
van Munster, Bertram
    Albuquerque International Balloon Fiesta and, 10–11
    in Amsterdam, 55
    filmmaking and producing experiences of, xiv–xv
    map of locations, 145
    production company of, xv, 85
    production team and, 147
    scouting locations, 102, 146
    travel experiences of, xiv–xv
Vatican City, Italy, 66

Vatnajökull National Park, Gardabaer, Iceland, 51
Venetian Masks, Venice, Italy, 64–65
Venice, Italy
    Gondola Ride, 63–64
    Make or Paint a Venetian Mask, 64–65
    other Venice must-sees, 64
Verzasca Dam, Gordola, Switzerland, 62
Victor Emmanuel II (king of Italy), 66
Victoria & Alfred Waterfront, Cape Town, South Africa, 89
Victoria (queen of England), 89
Victoria Falls, Zambia
    Fly in a Microlight Plane over Victoria Falls, 83–84
    Go on a Game Drive at Mosi-Oa-Tunya National Park, 84–85
    Run across Knife Edge at Victoria Falls, 83–84
Victoria Peak, Hong Kong, China, 113
Victoria Tower Gardens, London, United Kingdom, 48
Vienna, Austria
    Ride the Wiener Riesenrad (Giant Ferris Wheel in Vienna), 69–70
    Site where Beethoven wrote the Heiligenstadt Testament, 69
    Tour of Schönbrunn Palace, 68–69
Vietnam
    Ha Long Bay, 120–21
    Hanoi, 119–20
    Ho Chi Minh City, 122–24
Vietnam War, 119, 123
View the Taj Mahal from Mehtab Bagh (Moonlight Garden), Agra, India, 103
Villa Borghese, Rome, Italy, 66

Virtually Jump off the Tallest Skyscraper in the World, Dubai, United Arab Emirates, 92

visas, xvii

Vondelpark, Amsterdam, Netherlands, 56

W

Wadi Adventure River Rapids, Al Ain, United Arab Emirates, 100

Waitomo District, New Zealand, North Island, Go Spelunking at the Waitomo Caves, 138–39

walking shoes, xviii

Walk the Underground Sewers, Paris, France, 40–41

Walk through Hyde Park, Sydney, Australia, 133–34

Wasatch Mountains, Utah, 10

Washington Square Park, New York City, New York, 4

Watch a Live Polo Match, Buenos Aires, Argentina, 34

Wat Klang Food Market, Bangkok, Thailand, 128

"Welcome to Las Vegas" sign, Las Vegas, Nevada, 12

White, Jack, 6

Wiener Riesenrad (Giant Ferris Wheel in Vienna), Vienna, Austria, 69–70

Wild Things (wildlife series), xiii–xiv, 16, 85

Windmills of Kinderdijk, Netherlands, 56

Winter Olympic Games of 1924, 43

Winter Olympic Games of 1964, 68

Winter Olympic Games of 1976, 67–68

Winter Olympic Games of 1988, 21

Winter Olympic Games of 1998, 118

Wooden Bench at Promenade de la Treille, Geneva, Switzerland, 60

Worldrace Productions, xv

Wrigley Field, Chicago, Illinois, 8–9

X

Xi'an, China
Museum of Qin Terra-Cotta Warriors and Horses, 110–11
Take a Cable Car up Mount Hua and Place a Lock on the Railing, 111–12

Y

Yedikule Fortress, Istanbul, Turkey, 71

Yeni Mosque (the New Mosque), Istanbul, Turkey, 71

Yogyakarta, Indonesia, Descend 160 Feet into Jomblang Cave (Goa Jomblang), 129

Yongle Emperor (Ming Dynasty), 109–10

Yukuana people of Venezuela, x

Z

Zambia
Victoria Falls, 83–85
Zimbabwe Border, 86

Zanzibar, Tanzania
Darajani Market, 82
Freddie Mercury's childhood home, 81–82
Take a Ferry from Dar es Salaam to Zanzibar, 80
Visit Stone Town and Find the Royal Doors, 81

Zimbabwe Border, Zambia, Jump by Rope Swing into Batoka Gorge, 86

Zip-Lining at Cascada de las Ánimas, Santiago, Chile, 37–38

Zip-Lining down Holmenkollen Ski Jump, Oslo, Norway, 52–53

LEVEL UP YOUR VACATION WITH THE OFFICIAL COMPANION TO *THE AMAZING RACE.*

For more than twenty years, blockbuster reality show *The Amazing Race* has introduced millions to unique travel destinations in ninety-two countries across the globe, showcasing individual cultures with location-specific challenges for contestants.

Travel in the footsteps of contestants with this guide that covers six continents and thirty-two countries, including favorite activities and attractions for each. In addition to region-specific recommendations for destinations and activities from the show's history, *The Official Amazing Race Travel Companion* features never-before-seen behind-the-scenes snapshots of how the show is made, who the producers hire, and how destinations are chosen, along with a foreword by host Phil Keoghan.

The Official Amazing Race Travel Companion will satisfy any craving for adventure, whether you're an armchair traveler or about to hit the road!

ELISE DOGANIERI is a ten-time Emmy Award–winning co-producer and the executive producer of the CBS TV juggernaut *The Amazing Race*, which has also earned three Producers Guild of America Awards, a GLAAD Award, and a Television Critics Association Award. Elise lives in Los Angeles with her husband, Bertram van Munster, and their daughter, Ava.

TRAVEL   1022

ISBN 978-1-9821-7739-3   **$18.00 U.S./$25.00 Can.**

SimonandSchuster.com
🐦 📷 @_SimonElement

SIMON ELEMENT

COVER DESIGN BY PATRICK SULLIVAN

PRINTED IN THE U.S.A.

51800

9 781982 177393